M'Liss Rae Hawley's
Scrappy Quilts

Let the Fabric Tell Your Story

M'Liss Rae Hawley

C&T PUBLISHING

Text ©2008 by M'Liss Rae Hawley

Artwork: ©2008 by C&T Publishing, Inc.

Publisher: Amy Marson

Editorial Director: Gailen Runge

Acquisitions Editor: Jan Grigsby

Editor: Deb Rowden

Technical Editors: Carolyn Aune, Teresa Stroin, and Robyn Gronning

Copyeditor/Proofreader: Wordfirm Inc.

Cover Designer: Kristen Yenche

Book Designer: Kristen Yenche

Illustrator: John Heisch

Production Coordinator: Tim Manibusan

Photography: Luke Mulks and Diane Pedersen, unless otherwise noted

Author photo: Michael Stadler

Published by: C&T Publishing, Inc., P.O. Box 1456, Lafayette, CA 94549

Library of Congress Cataloging-in-Publication Data

Hawley, M'Liss Rae,

M'Liss Rae Hawley's scrappy quilts : let the fabric tell your story / M'Liss Rae Hawley.

p. cm.

Summary: "A guide to creating successful, multi-fabric (scrap) quilts. Covers selecting, preparing, and blending many fabrics for pleasing results, with focus on understanding the tools of color, value, and print. Includes 8 projects with a gallery of work to support each pattern"--Provided by publisher.

ISBN 978-1-57120-442-4 (paper trade : alk. paper)

1. Patchwork--Patterns. 2. Quilting--Patterns. I. Title.

TT835H347135 2008

746.46'041--dc22

2007037336

Printed in China

10 9 8 7 6 5 4 3 2 1

Dedication

I would like to express my deep appreciation to my group of contributors. For many years, we have met regularly at Useless Bay Golf and Country Club on Whidbey Island. While there, we eat great food, share ideas and fabric, and laugh through the many joys and challenges of books and life.

Annette Barca	Susie Kincy
Barbara Dau	Marie Miller
Vicki DeGraaf	Lucia Pan
John James	Anastasia Riordan
Louise James	Leslie Rommann
Peggy Johnson	Carla Zimmermann

Acknowledgments

I would like to gratefully thank the following people and companies that share my vision, enthusiasm, and love of quilting and have contributed to the creation of this book.

C&T Publishing: Amy Marson, Jan Grigsby, Darra Williamson, Deb Rowden, Carolyn Aune, Teresa Stroin, Kris Yenche, Tim Manibusan, and all the staff that continue to create wonderful books.

Electric Quilt

Hoffman Fabrics

Husqvarna Viking

Jo-Ann Fabric and Craft Stores

Quilters Dream Batting

Robison-Anton Textiles

Sulky of America

Vicki DeGraaf, my best friend: She's had a quilt in every book I've written and continues to help with cutting, piecing, and binding!

Peggy Johnson, the Keeper of the Blocks and best friend: With the Electric Quilt software, Peggy helped draft the quilts in this book.

Susie Kincy, my assistant and best friend: She's always ready to help with whatever I need! Erin Rae Vautier, my sister and best friend: She's always available to help bind quilts!

Darra Williamson, my editor and friend: We've worked on seven books together!

Michael Stadler, my photographer and friend. We've done dozens of photo shoots together; thank you for your patience with me, all the dachshunds, and the girls! You are an amazing photographer!

Finally, thank you to Michael and Adrienne. They wash and iron fabric, carry suitcases all over the world, prepare food, and continue to love and support me!

Contents

Introduction **4**

It's All about the Fabric **6**

How-Tos **13**

The Projects

Parade **22**

Parade: Version II **26**

Focus on a Theme **29**

Embroidered Expressions **38**

Shooting Star **46**

Fence Rail **55**

Fence Rail: Version II **59**

Scrappy Kaleidoscope **64**

Gathering Moments **72**

Gathering Moments on Point: Version II **76**

Union Square **83**

Union Square: Pillows and Pillowcases **87**

Union Square: Version II **90**

Resources **94**

About the Author **95**

Introduction

What is a scrap quilt? Ask ten quilters and you'll get ten different answers.

Some say that a quilt is a scrap quilt when every fabric used is a leftover from another sewing project. Some say that for a quilt to be considered a scrap quilt, it must contain at least 50 or 100 or 200 different fabrics. Some say every block in a scrap quilt must include a different combination of fabrics.

Truth is, all of these definitions might be correct . . . as may a dozen more. Quilters have been making quilts from small amounts of a wide variety of fabrics for more than 200 years. Depending on the economic status or sentimentality of the maker, these fabrics might be scavenged from worn-out clothing or household textiles, accumulated over time by collecting or trading with friends, purchased brand-new for quiltmaking, or gathered from a combination of sources. Blocks may pair a common background with different foreground pieces, may be made with different background *and* foreground fabrics, or may use a different fabric for *every* piece in *every* block. In each case, the quilt might reasonably be called a scrap quilt.

The one thing upon which all agree is that a scrap quilt involves using *many* fabrics. For quiltmakers, who are fabric lovers by nature, that is where the fun begins.

Nowadays, we are lucky to have an unprecedented selection of fabrics at our fingertips: fabrics in every color and print imaginable, unique pieces imported from countries all over the world, and carefully researched prints reproduced from various periods in quiltmaking's history. With such abundance, it is certainly possible to make our quilts, including our "scrap" quilts, entirely with fabric purchased specifically for this purpose. But that is only *half* the fun.

In a sense, the fusion of old and new is the true attraction of scrap quilts. A scrap quilt provides a great opportunity to include cherished fabrics: bits and pieces left from clothing you wore as a child, remnants of clothing or nursery accessories you made or have saved from your children or grandchildren, snippets of vintage fabric from your grandma's sewing room. Because you need only small amounts of any one fabric for a scrap quilt, you can combine these treasures with pieces from your stash: perhaps the remaining inches from a longtime and much-used favorite or from a fabric so beautiful you couldn't bear to cut it. By using just a small square, strip, or motif, you will always have a reminder of the unique story behind the fabric. When you combine these fabric memories with the resources available now from the shelves of quilt and fabric stores and over the Internet, the possibilities are truly endless.

Of course, how these elements are combined is what makes the difference. While much of the early history of scrap quilts was about wasting nothing and making do, we have the opportunity and the means today to change the focus from simply making do to making art, while still paying homage to the traditional source. We can take the idea of the scrap quilt—that is, the combination of many, many different fabrics—merge it with new innovations, such as machine embroidery and embellishment, and apply it to the creation of something truly unique and beautiful. We can focus on color and design—the two qualities that I consider the path to creativity. This approach requires time for gathering fabrics you *really* like, using them to create visually appealing blocks or strata, and carefully placing them as part of an overall design in a creative experience that I call "seeking solutions."

I'd like you to view this book as a guide for your creative journey. Look through the pages, study and be inspired by the many beautiful and diverse quilts and styles, and find your comfort zone. The projects are arranged by degree of difficulty, with the easiest first and the more difficult at the end. Choose your favorite pattern and give it a try, perhaps in one of its smaller versions. Forge ahead with confidence, with reckless abandon. Making a scrap quilt is not difficult. It is *fun,* and I can almost guarantee that you'll stretch as a quiltmaker for having made it. In fact, I'll bet you can't stop at making just one!

Enjoy the journey,

◆ The blocks in my quilt *The Magic Hour* include scraps of fabrics from the first dress I ever made (as a nine-year-old!) and from curtains that were hanging in my family's home when I was born. For a full view of this quilt—and instructions for making your own Scrappy Kaleidoscope quilt—see page 64.

It's All about the Fabric

I am passionate about everything to do with quilting, beginning with choosing the fabrics. Admittedly, I have a vast fabric collection. But let's face it: nothing brings quilters more joy than adding to their existing stash. The more fabric you have to select from—especially when you are making scrap quilts—the more creative you can be.

So, pull out those fabrics you have accumulated over a lifetime—I suspect you'll discover that this process is like visiting with old friends, recalling pleasant memories of previous quilts, crafts, and clothing projects—but don't stop there! Combine these pieces with new fabrics to achieve the look you want.

Scrap quilts are a great way to infuse a fresh, new perspective in your work. Think about mixing colors, prints, and textures you wouldn't normally use, or use them in a particular combination. Create challenges for yourself. Working with your quilting friends or quilt guild can motivate you to try new and exciting blends.

The only downside to making a scrap quilt is putting the leftover fabric away when you are finished. (Making scrap quilts doesn't seem to dent your fabric stash as much as you might think. Ask any scrap quilter!) But it's a small price to pay for an exhilarating and liberating experience—and a new quilt besides—don't you agree?

the language and process of scrap quilts

A great scrap quilt is not an accident. As with any other quilt, it requires careful planning and forethought—perhaps even more so, since there are so many variables involved.

Don't be afraid to take a creative risk. Creativity is the essence of life. Creating and re-creating keeps us alive—whether we are painting our home, planting a garden, preparing a meal, or making a quilt.

Here's an overview of how I break down the steps—in essence, the language and process of making a scrap quilt.

Planning   This is your starting point—the point at which you find your inspiration in a color scheme, a favorite fabric or collection of fabrics, a theme, a photograph, or an antique quilt. Sometimes a particular pattern will provide the inspiration. I've included eight patterns in this book to get you started. Now is the time to select the pattern you wish to use and to decide whether you want to work with true "scraps" (leftovers from other projects), with purchased fabrics (either already in or added now to your stash), or with a combination of the two. The size of your scrap bag and the vision for your quilt will help you decide which path to take.

Carla Zimmermann was inspired by her collection of Civil War–era reproduction fabrics to make *Stars Watch Over Civil War Battlefield,* her version of the Union Square quilt. See page 92 for a full view.

Gathering Once you determine your vision of the quilt, you are ready to gather the fabrics to implement that vision. Keep in mind the quilt's end use; that is, will it be used on a bed and ultimately laundered, or displayed on a wall, which means nontraditional fabrics (e.g., silk, corduroy, velvet) are an option?

Start by reviewing your current resources—your existing fabric collection. Don't overlook the leftovers from previous projects, including strips (1½″ precut or otherwise), strip sets or strata, cutaway triangles from sew-and-flip techniques, and so on. Supplement by swapping and sharing with friends. If your plans include vintage fabrics, visit garage sales or flea markets. Finally, go shopping to add some fresh new fabrics to your choices. Fat quarters are a good way to build or supplement a broad fabric "paint box."

YOU'VE GOT TO HAVE FRIENDS!

Sharing and trading with friends is a win-win way to add to your fabric stash. When purchasing fabric, I often buy fat quarters in duplicate—one for me and one to trade. Another option is to buy ⅝ yard, which gives you a fat quarter to trade and ⅜ yard to keep. This ⅜ yard is enough for a fat quarter, a 1½″ strip for my collection, and a tiny bit extra.

Developing This is the actual construction phase: cutting the shapes; assembling the strata, units, and blocks; determining a setting and border treatment; and so on. Don't rush this process. Use your design wall to audition and edit.

Be an observer. Observation is an important element in creativity. Live with your quilt for a while in its various stages, viewing it over the course of a few days, perhaps even at different times of the day. Stay alert and involved as the quilt emerges. Opportunities will continue to present themselves at each step of the process.

Finishing The challenge at this stage is to keep the momentum going, to move forward and make final decisions, and to finish your quilt!

choosing your fabrics

The fabrics you choose for your scrap quilt will help establish a look, a mood, or an impression for your quilt. It might be traditional, formal, lighthearted, opulent, contemporary, classic, vintage, edgy . . . the list goes on and on. But where to begin?

A logical place to start is with a color or colors you like. To expand your horizons, get out your color wheel and use it as a guide for choosing other colors. (For more on the color wheel and how it works, refer to *Get Creative with M'Liss Rae Hawley*; see Resources on page 94.) You may find some unusual combinations, possibly including colors that are not your favorites. You'll be surprised to see the impact these colors can make, especially when used in small amounts, as for an accent. (More on that later.)

Each quilter, as an artist, brings his or her own life experiences to a quilt, favoring certain colors or patterns while reacting negatively to others. Whatever your taste, there are three key elements to consider when making fabric choices for your scrap quilt:

- Color
- Value
- Visual texture—texture, scale, and style of print

You'll need a good mix of each for a successful outcome.

Color

The inspiration for your palette can come from any number of places. Sometimes I select a favorite color and then use the color wheel to find compatible companions. Sometimes the inspiration comes from a particular fabric or group of fabrics I want to include. Sometimes I'm inspired by a particular look or mood or era I want to suggest.

As you make *your* choices, remember that color families are large—ranging from the lightest tints to the darkest shades. Don't be afraid to use them all in your scrap quilt.

Fabric families are large—don't forget to include all the members!

Once you've determined your color scheme, collect every fabric in your stash, including scraps, that falls within that palette. Expand your choices by adding vintage fabrics, fabrics you've gathered by trading with friends, and fabrics newly added to your collection.

Don't worry now if all the fabrics match. You may not—and probably won't—use them all in the final quilt. However, the more you have to start with, the wider your choices, and the more fabrics of a color you use in your quilt, the more likely the fabrics are to blend.

Quilters sometimes include neutral fabrics in their quilts, often using them as backgrounds. Neutrals are especially useful in scrap quilts, as they help unify the many colors, values, and prints.

A true neutral is white, gray, or black. Most people also consider off-white (in its many variations, including cream, ivory, and ecru), beige, tan, and brown as neutrals. However, I like to think that quilters can take liberty and add their own personal "neutrals" to the standard list. I have three personal neutrals: yellow, green, and pink. Your neutral may simply be the lightest value of your favorite color.

Traditional neutrals

Quilters' neutrals

My personal neutrals

Don't forget to include an accent color in your choice of fabrics. An accent is typically used in small amounts to add a little sparkle—something unexpected. Your accent might be a brighter, more intense version of a color you are already using—for example, fuchsia with reds, sunflower gold with yellow-orange, or rich aqua with blue-green. Another idea is to go back to the color wheel. Often one of the colors in your color scheme—sometimes your less-than-favorite color—makes the perfect accent when used in small amounts.

Something seems to be missing here.
The colors seem a little flat.

The same fabrics spiced up with an accent color—much better!

Value

Value refers to the lightness or darkness of a color in relationship to those around it. It is an essential factor in the success of your quilt. Value creates contrast and allows the pattern to emerge.

Even if you make a one-color (monochromatic) quilt, the range of values within that single color is what makes the quilt work. See *Look at All Those Blues* by Annette Barca (page 92) for an example of a scrappy monochromatic quilt.

Strive for a good mix of visual textures.

DRAMATIC BACKGROUNDS

The background of your quilt doesn't always need to be the lightest fabric. I used my darkest fabrics in the block backgrounds for my quilt *In the Limelight* (page 46), with dramatic results.

For a bit of the unexpected,
try using dark background fabrics.

Stripes

Visual Texture

In general, the wider the variety of print types, the better. Too much of the same thing blends into an uninteresting, indistinguishable "gray" mush.

Mix it up with florals, paisleys, stripes, plaids, feathers, dots, and novelty (theme) prints. Vary the print scale from large to small, the repeat from random to regular, and the motifs from airy to tightly packed.

Florals

Geometrics

Include small- and large-scale prints in each print category.

Select fabrics with both regular and random repeating motifs.

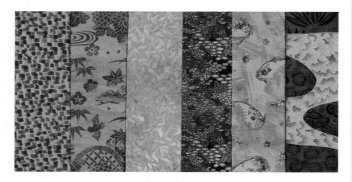

Balance dense, tightly packed prints with those that include some "breathing room."

Of course, every "rule" has its exception. If you look closely at my quilt *I Love Life!* (see page 55), you'll notice that all of the fabrics are batiks. There is enough variety in color and value—and even a little difference in the visual texture of some of the fabrics—to carry the quilt. This is a perfect example of what I call "reducing your variables," even in a scrap quilt!

ENHANCE WITH THREAD AND TRIM

You can supplement your color scheme not just with fabrics, but also with the threads you use for embroidery quilting, as well as with any fibers, beads, buttons, or other trims you include as embellishment. Embellishments can be new or vintage, so long as they complement the overall quilt design.

working with multiple fabrics

When it comes to scrap quilts, there are no rules other than the ones you create for yourself. The good news is that those rules can change from project to project. Your only task is to create a balance, to find harmony among disparate fabrics.

As I mentioned, there are a number of ways to approach a scrap quilt. You may decide to combine a single background fabric with a collection of different foreground pieces, as Leslie Rommann did in *Star Pinwheel* (page 52). You may prefer to use different background fabrics while keeping them in the same color family, as John and Louise James did in their version of the same pattern, *Autumn Stars* (page 51). You may decide to go totally scrappy and cut your fabrics—even within a single block—from a wide variety of prints, as Susie Kincy did in *Grandmother's Button Baskets* (page 81).

As long as the value remains consistent, it doesn't matter if the colors change. If there is enough contrast, the foreground—that is, the pattern—will remain distinct.

The same goes for the foreground fabrics. For example, you might repeat the same color of fabric in a specific spot in each block, as I did in the center of the star blocks for *In the Limelight* (page 46). Or you can let go and make the mix as scrappy as you please. The decision is up to you.

My Scrappy Kaleidoscope quilt *The Magic Hour* (page 64; detail on page 5) is a good example of a quilt with a no-holds-barred scrappy mix. For this quilt, I wanted to use as many different fabrics as possible from my fabric "history." The quilt includes fabrics of just about every theme and visual texture imaginable—more than 300 prints in all. (If you've been quilting awhile, you'll probably recognize some golden oldies!) I approached each strata as a single unique piece of artwork, with few duplications.

In photography, there is a special time in the evening called *the magic hour.* For my quilt, I planned from the beginning to capture this special time when the day turns to evening. Each fabric in the strata and cornerstones was placed to carry out this theme.

With so many fabrics in the quilt body, you will probably want to keep the borders fairly simple. For *The Magic Hour,* I used a black ikat with red highlights. This doesn't mean, however, that you can't choose a terrific print for your border. Experiment. Try a variety of fabrics to find the best choice. If you use a print border, try adding a plain inner border to frame the quilt center. If your design warrants it, consider forgoing a border altogether, a choice very much in keeping with the scrap quilts of the nineteenth century.

You'll find lots of creative options scattered throughout the book—in the words that introduce each project, as well as within the projects themselves in the form of tips and sidebars. Don't be afraid to try an idea suggested for one project on another quilt. Stay open to the possibilities.

preparing the fabric

I advocate prewashing all newly purchased fabrics to preshrink them and to remove excess dye and any chemicals used in the finishing process. I generally wash new fabrics as soon as I bring them into the house. That way, there is never any doubt as to whether a fabric has been laundered when I pull it from my shelf to use in a quilt.

I wash fat quarters or smaller pieces in the sink and larger pieces in the washing machine. All pieces go into the dryer, and then the family steps in to help: my husband, Michael, presses the fabric, and I square it up (see Rotary Cutting on page 13) and cut off a 1½″ strip (see You've Got to Have Friends! on page 7) with the help of our daughter, Adrienne. The fabric is on the shelf in no time.

LITTLE PIECES!

When working with scraps, you may not know whether they have been prewashed. If you expect the finished quilt will be laundered, you should wash these small pieces just in case. You don't want them to shrink in the finished quilt and distort the surface.

Hand wash small pieces in the sink, or, if you prefer, place them in a mesh bag and wash them in the washing machine with your other fabrics. Spread out the scraps to air dry or press them dry with a hot iron.

storing your fabrics

Having a large collection of fabrics to choose from, including lots of scraps and small pieces, is a wonderful thing; however, finding an efficient way to store it can be a challenge! The key consideration in establishing a storage system is that the fabric *must be accessible*. Storing it in the attic, garage, or basement (or for some quilters, the storage unit!) is fine if that is where you typically work, but otherwise doing so might limit your creativity. You must be able to get to your fabric! If you can't see it or reach it, you won't use it . . . and that would be a shame.

Different quilters sort their fabrics by different categories. Again, choose a system that works for you. You may prefer to sort your yardages, fat quarters, and scraps by color, by value, by type of print, or by some combination of criteria.

Once you've determined your sorting system, you can then decide how to store the fabrics. Closets, shelving (protected from direct light to avoid fabric fading), trunks, bureaus, and other chests are possibilities for larger pieces. Browse your local home improvement center for ideas of preassembled or assemble-it-yourself modular storage systems.

Smaller pieces can be stashed in plastic or rubber tubs and containers, in baskets, or even in suitcases. Check your favorite container outlet or website for ideas.

LETTING GO

A fabric collection is a fluid thing, and there occasionally comes a time when you need to reassess your "holdings." As you rethink your fabric storage or begin to make fabric selections for a scrap quilt, you will likely come across fabric that you know you will never use. Maybe the fabric has not aged well—the dye has faded, the color is dated, or you've simply outgrown it. Perhaps, in your enthusiasm, you bought 3 yards when 1 yard was plenty. Why not winnow these fabrics out now and ease your storage situation?

Many individuals and groups are eager to have your fabric. Fabric that you've overestimated or outgrown might make a good start on a stash for a new quilter. Schools, camps, youth and church groups, and senior citizen centers are often grateful for fabrics to use in craft projects. Ask around. You may be surprised at the number of willing takers.

How-Tos

Here are some tips and techniques designed to make the scrap quilt experience both fun and successful. For more detailed information about the basics of quiltmaking, refer to *Making Your First Quilt with M'Liss Rae Hawley* (see Resources on page 94).

rotary cutting

Almost all the pieces for the quilts in this book can be cut with a rotary cutter. It is essential that you square the edges of your fabrics before you rotary cut them into strips and pieces. The fabric edges must be straight for the resulting pieces to be straight. Make sure the fabric is pressed and that you fold it carefully before you begin cutting. If you have a large piece of yardage, fold it twice or break it down so that you can work with a more manageable amount.

Note: Cutting instructions are for right-handers. Reverse if you are left-handed.

1. Place the folded fabric on the cutting mat, with the fold closest to you.

2. Position your ruler on the right edge of the fabric so that the ruler is perpendicular to the fold. Trim a narrow strip from the right edge of the fabric to square it up.

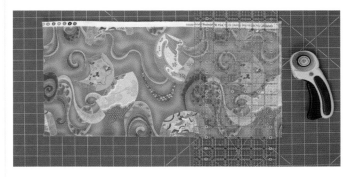

3. Rotate the fabric (or the mat) 180° and repeat Step 2 at the opposite edge.

Cutting Strips and Pieces

Whether you are cutting scraps, small pieces such as fat quarters, or yardage, use the lines on your ruler, not on your mat, to measure and cut. Use the mat grid only for aligning the fabric and taking rough measurements.

1. Working from the squared left edge of the fabric, measure and cut a strip the desired width. Repeat to cut the required number of strips. You may need to square up the end after every few cuts.

2. Cut the strips into squares or other smaller segments as directed in the project instructions.

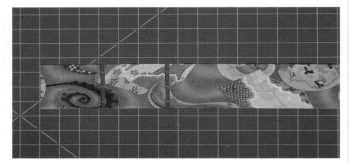

Although a half-square triangle and a quarter-square triangle look the same, there is one key difference. In a half-square triangle, the straight grain (lengthwise and crosswise) falls on the two short sides of the shape, and the long diagonal edge falls on the stretchy bias. With a quarter-square triangle, the long diagonal edge falls on the straight grain (lengthwise or crosswise), while the stretchy bias falls on the two short sides.

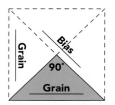 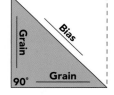

Quarter-square triangle   Half-square triangle

Whether you cut half- or quarter-square triangles will depend on where you want the straight grain of the triangle to fall in the unit or block. In most cases, this will be on the outside edge. In any case, begin by cutting squares as described above. Then follow the steps below.

To make half-square triangles, use your rotary cutter and ruler to divide each square from corner to corner in one direction, as shown. Each square yields two half-square triangles with the straight grain (lengthwise and crosswise) on the two short sides.

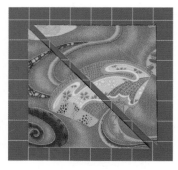

Half-square triangle

To make quarter-square triangles, use your rotary cutter and ruler to divide each square from corner to corner in **both** directions, as shown. Each square yields four quarter-square triangles with the straight of grain (lengthwise or crosswise) on the long diagonal side.

Quarter-square triangle

piecing and pressing

Unless noted otherwise, use a ¼˝ seam allowance for piecing the quilts in this book. It's always a good idea to check that your ¼˝ seam is accurate before beginning to sew.

For the projects in this book, the direction to press the seams will be indicated either in the instructions themselves or by arrows in the accompanying diagrams. Press lightly with a lifting-and-lowering motion. Dragging the iron across the fabric can distort the individual pieces and the finished blocks.

adding borders

The quilts in this book include two different border treatments: squared borders and mitered borders.

Squared Borders

Squared borders are the easiest of all borders. In most cases, you will be directed to stitch the top and bottom borders first. If the quilt top is slightly longer than the border, stitch with the quilt top on the bottom, closest to the feed dogs. If the reverse is true, stitch with the border on the bottom. The motion of the feed dogs will help ease in the extra length.

1. Measure the finished quilt top through the center from side to side. Cut 2 borders to this measurement. These will be the top and bottom borders.

2. Place pins at the center points of the top and bottom of the quilt top, as well as at the center point of each border strip. Pin the borders to the quilt top, matching the ends and center points. Use additional pins as needed, easing or gently stretching the border to fit. Sew the borders to the quilt top with a ¼˝ seam allowance. Press as instructed—usually toward the borders.

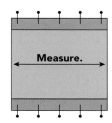

3. Measure the quilt from top to bottom, including the borders you've just sewn. Cut 2 borders to this measurement. These will be the side borders. Repeat Step 2 to pin, sew, and press the borders.

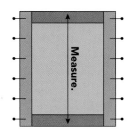

Borders with Cornerstones

The instructions for *Gathering Love* (page 76) include borders with cornerstones. Some of the other quilts include this option as well.

1. Measure the quilt top through the center from side to side and from top to bottom. Cut 2 borders to each of these measurements.

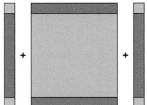

2. Sew the appropriately sized strips to the top and bottom of the quilt. Press the seams toward the borders. Sew a cornerstone to each end of the remaining borders. Press the seams toward the borders. Sew the border units to the sides of the quilt and press the seams toward the borders.

Mitered Borders

1. Measure the finished quilt top through the center from top to bottom to find the length of the quilt. To this measurement, add 2 times the width of the border plus approximately 5˝. Cut 2 borders to this measurement. These will be the *side* borders.

2. Measure the finished quilt top from side to side to find the width of the quilt. To this measurement, add 2 times the width of the border plus approximately 5˝. Cut 2 borders to this measurement. These will be the *top and bottom* borders.

3. Place pins to mark the midpoints of all sides of the quilt top, as well as the midpoint of each border strip.

4. Measure and pin-mark *half the length* of the quilt top on both sides of the midpoint pin on each side border strip. Pin the borders to the sides of the quilt, matching the pins at the midpoints and the pins marking the quilt length to the edges of the quilt top. (The excess border length will extend beyond each edge of the quilt.)

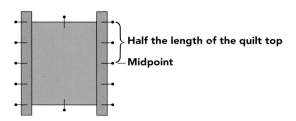

Half the length of the quilt top

Midpoint

5. Stitch the border strips to the sides of the quilt, stopping ¼˝ from the edge of the quilt with a backstitch. Press the seams toward the borders.

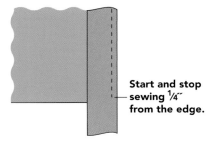

Start and stop sewing ¼˝ from the edge.

6. Measure and pin-mark *half the width* of the quilt top on either side of the midpoint pins on the top and bottom border strips. Pin the borders to the top and bottom of the quilt, matching the pins at the midpoints and the pins marking the quilt width to the edges of the quilt. (The excess border length will extend beyond each edge of the quilt.) Repeat Step 5 to sew the top and bottom borders to the quilt.

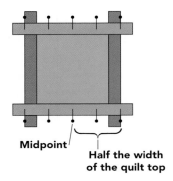

Midpoint

Half the width of the quilt top

7. To create the miter, place a corner of the quilt right side up on your ironing board. Place the excess tail of one of the border strips on top of the adjacent border strip.

8. Fold the top border strip under at a 45° angle so that it meets the edge of the bottom border strip. Lightly press the fold in place. Use a ruler or right-angle triangle to be certain that the angle is correct and that the corner is square. Press the fold again, firmly this time.

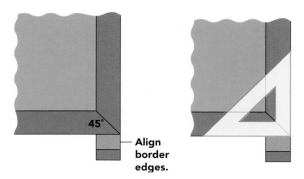

45°

Align border edges.

9. Fold the quilt top diagonally with right sides together and align the long edges of the border strips. Place pins near the pressed fold to secure the corners of the border strips for sewing.

10. Beginning with a backstitch at the inside corner of the border, carefully stitch toward the outside edge along the fold. Finish with a backstitch.

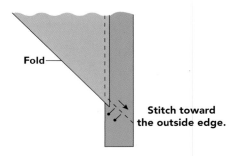

Fold

Stitch toward the outside edge.

11. Trim the seam allowance to ¼″ and press the seam open.

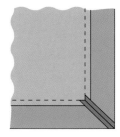

preparing your quilt for quilting

Don't skimp in preparing your quilt for quilting! Take the time to layer it properly and baste it sufficiently. The result—a quilt free of puckers and bumps—will make you proud.

Batting and Backing

The choice of batting is a personal decision, but you'll want to consider the method (and amount) of quilting you plan to do, as well as the quilt's end use. Because I prefer machine quilting, I usually use cotton batting in a heavier weight for bed quilts and wallhangings and in a lighter weight for clothing. You'll probably want to stick with lightweight batting for hand quilting. Polyester batting is a good choice for tied quilts.

No matter which type of batting you choose, cut the batting approximately 4″ larger than the quilt top on all sides.

As with the batting, you'll want the quilt backing to be approximately 4″ larger than the quilt top on all sides. You'll sometimes need to piece the fabric to have a large enough backing piece. I piece my backing so that the seams run vertically. The yardage specified in the projects is enough for vertical seams. Be sure to prewash the backing fabric and remove the selvages first.

Layering and Basting

Unlike many machine quilters, I prefer to hand baste with thread rather than pin baste. This allows me to machine quilt without having to stop to remove pins.

1. Carefully press the quilt top from the back to set the seams and then press from the front. Press the backing. If you wish, use spray starch or sizing.

2. Spread the backing wrong side up on a clean, flat surface and secure it with masking tape. The fabric should be taut but not stretched. Center the batting over the backing. Finally, center the quilt top over the batting.

3. Thread a long needle with light-colored thread. Beginning in the center of the quilt, stitch a 4″ grid of horizontal and vertical lines.

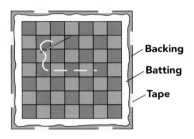

4. When you've finished basting, remove the tape and get ready to quilt.

quilting your quilt

A quilt becomes a quilt when it includes three layers—a top, a layer of batting, and a backing—all secured with stitching of some type to hold the layers together. (This means that to call your project a quilt, you need to finish it!) Some quilters create that stitching by hand; others, by machine. My quilts in this book—as well as almost all the quilts made by my wonderful group of quilters—were machine quilted.

Each step of the quiltmaking process, including the machine quilting, is exciting and fun to me. I love the idea of adding yet another level of creativity to my quilts. Machine quilting my own tops gives me flexibility in making those design decisions, and I do my own quilting whenever I can. Because of time constraints, however, I find I must now have many of my quilt tops professionally machine quilted. If you have stacks of quilt tops waiting to be quilted, you might want to consider that option.

Machine quilting is an art form, so there is a learning curve involved. Practice is the best way to learn and master this skill. Here are some guidelines to get you started.

Dual-Feed Foot

The dual-feed foot is designed to hold and feed the three layers of your quilt evenly as you stitch. Use this foot to machine quilt single lines or parallel lines and grids, whether vertical, horizontal, or diagonal. You can also use this foot for certain decorative stitches and embellishing techniques, such as couching.

Dual-feed foot

Open-Toe Stippling Foot

Also called a darning foot, the open-toe stippling foot allows you to quilt in all directions—you are the guide! Use this foot for stipple quilting, meandering, and other free-motion techniques. I like to stipple quilt around machine-embroidered motifs, because this causes the embroidered design to pop out and become a focal point.

You will need to drop the feed dogs on your sewing machine when you use the open-toe stippling foot. You might also need to set the presser foot pressure to the darning position so you can move the quilt at a smooth pace for consistent stitches. Some machines have a built-in stipple stitch, which is a wonderful way to achieve this beautiful surface texture.

Open-toe stippling foot

Threads

I consider quilting thread to be a design element, not just the means to hold the three layers of my quilts together. I also believe that variety in thread adds visual interest and showcases the quilter's individuality. For these reasons, I frequently use a mix of threads in my quilts. When choosing thread, I consider thread color, texture, and weight as well as where I plan to use the thread.

Typical thread choices for machine quilting include rayon (35- and 40-weight), cotton, polyester, and monofilament. I use a lot of variegated and metallic threads, as well as novelty threads, such as Twister Tweeds, Swirling Sensation, and Moon Glow (see Resources on page 94).

Design

Let your imagination be your guide in choosing quilting motifs for your scrappy quilts. Design sources are everywhere! Look carefully at quilts in museums, shows, books, and magazines; at books of quilting patterns; and at quilting stencils. Observe patterns in other areas of your life—particularly patterns in nature.

Begin by anchoring key seams in and around blocks and borders by stitching in the ditch along the seamlines. Try filling in open spaces with loops, curves, clamshells, and waves. Combine straight and curvy lines for variety.

I love to use heavy free-motion quilting, such as stippling, in the backgrounds behind pieced, appliquéd, and embroidered motifs. Heavy quilting causes the background to recede and the motif to pop forward, giving it center stage in the design.

Note how the heavily quilted background in this block of *Coi Dragon* (page 38) makes the embroidery seem to pop.

HAVING YOUR QUILT MACHINE QUILTED

Turning your precious quilt top over to a professional machine quilter can be pretty daunting, but it doesn't need to be! Consider yourself and your machine quilter a team; don't hesitate to make your thoughts, preferences, and suggestions known.

Spend some time before you deliver your quilt top doing research about quilting motifs and threads you would like the quilter to use. Make sure you schedule your drop-off at a time when you are both available to sit down and discuss

these key decisions. If possible, bring along sketches, photographs, books, magazines, stencils, or other examples, while at the same time staying open to any suggestions your quilter may have. If you envision a particular color or type of thread (e.g., bright red, variegated, rayon, metallic, even invisible), discuss this with your quilter and provide the materials as necessary. Don't forget to address batting, backing, and finishing as well.

One of my favorite options is to let the fabric inspire me. I can stitch a garden trellis over a floral fabric or add detail to a beach with quilted rocks and shells. I also love to pull a motif from the fabric and adapt it for quilting in another area of the quilt. A simpler option is to follow the fabric motif right where it is. The latter option is especially effective in a large-scale background fabric or outer-border fabric.

finishing your quilt

The binding, hanging sleeve, and label of your quilt are important too, so be sure to give them the same attention you've given to every other element.

Squaring Up

Before adding the binding, you need to trim the excess batting and backing and square up your quilt. Use the seams of the outer borders as a guide.

1. Align a ruler with the outer-border seam and measure to the edge of the quilt in several places. Use the narrowest measurement as a guide for positioning your ruler. Trim the excess batting and backing all around the quilt.

2. Fold the quilt in half lengthwise and crosswise to check that the corners are square and that the sides are equal in length. If they aren't, use a large square ruler to even them up, one corner at a time.

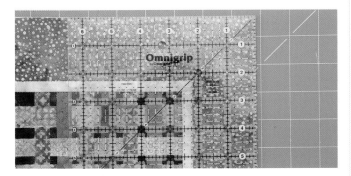

3. Stabilize the quilt edges by stitching around the perimeter with a basting or serpentine stitch. (Do not use a zigzag stitch, as it can push and pull the fabric out of shape.)

4. Remove any stray threads or bits of batting from the quilt top. You are now ready to bind your quilt.

Making and Applying Binding

Binding is an important and, sadly, often overlooked step in the quiltmaking process. Many a wonderful quilt is spoiled by a poorly sewn binding. Take your time deciding what fabric you will use and enjoy the process of stitching it to your quilt. You're coming down the home stretch now!

Typically, I cut binding strips 3″ wide from selvage to selvage across the width of the fabric. I make an exception and cut strips on the bias only when I want to create a special effect with a plaid or striped fabric or when I need to follow a curved or rounded edge.

I use the following method to bind my quilts. It results in a finished edge that is attractive and strong.

1. Cut enough binding strips to go around the perimeter (outside edges) of the quilt plus an extra 10″ for seams and corners. Sew the strips together at right angles, as shown. Trim the excess fabric from the seams, leaving a ¼″ seam allowance, and press the seams open.

2. Fold the binding in half lengthwise, wrong sides together, and press.

3. Starting 6″ down from the upper-right corner and with the raw edges even, place the binding on the quilt top. Check to see that none of the diagonal seams falls on a corner of the quilt. If one does, adjust the starting point. Begin stitching 4″ from the end of the binding, using a ½″ seam allowance.

4. Stitch about 2″ and then stop and cut the threads. Remove the quilt from the machine and fold the binding to the back of the quilt. The binding should cover the line of machine stitching on the back. If the binding overlaps the stitching too much, try again, taking a slightly wider seam allowance. If the binding doesn't cover the original line of stitching, take a slightly narrower seam allowance. Remove the unwanted stitches before you continue.

5. Using the stitching position you determined in Step 4, resume stitching until you are ½″ from the first corner of the quilt. Stop, backstitch, cut the thread, and remove the quilt from the machine.

6. Fold the binding straight up at a 45° angle and then down to create a mitered corner.

7. Resume stitching, mitering each corner as you come to it.

8. Stop stitching about 3″ after you've turned the last corner. Make sure the starting and finishing ends of the binding overlap by at least 4″. Cut the threads and remove the quilt from the machine. Measure a 3″ overlap and trim the excess binding.

9. Place the quilt right side up. Unfold the unstitched binding tails, place them right sides together at right angles, and pin them together. Draw a line from the upper-left corner to the lower-right corner of the binding and stitch on the drawn line.

10. Carefully trim the seam allowance to ¼″ and press the seam open. Refold the binding and press. Finish stitching the binding to the quilt.

11. Turn the binding to the back of the quilt and pin it. (I pin approximately 12″ at a time.) Use matching-colored thread to blindstitch the binding to the quilt back, carefully mitering the corners as you approach them. Hand stitch the miters on both sides.

Making and Adding a Sleeve

If you want to display your quilt on a wall, you need to add a sleeve to protect your work of art from excessive strain.

1. Cut an 8½″-wide strip of backing fabric 1″ shorter than the width of the quilt. (If the quilt is wider than 40″, cut 2 strips and stitch them together end to end.) Fold under the short ends ¼″. Stitch and press.

2. Fold the sleeve in half lengthwise, right sides together. Sew the long raw edges together and press the seam open. Turn the sleeve right side out and press again.

3. Mark the midpoint of the sleeve and the midpoint of the top edge of the quilt. Align the midpoints and pin the sleeve to the quilt, right below the binding. Use matching-colored thread to blindstitch the top edge in place.

4. Push up the bottom edge of the sleeve a tiny bit so that when the hanging rod is inserted, it will not put strain on the quilt. Blindstitch the bottom edge of the sleeve, taking care not to catch the front of the quilt as you stitch.

Creating a Label

I always recommend making a label for your quilt. A label gives you a place to provide important information about both you and the quilt. I like to make my labels large—about 4″ × 7″—so I have plenty of room. You can sew the label to the lower-right corner of the quilt back before it is quilted or wait to attach the label after you have completed the quilt.

I suggest including the following information on your label: the name of the quilt; your full name (and business name, if you have one); your city, county, province or state, and country of residence; and the date.

If the quilt was made for a special person, to commemorate a special event, or as part of a series, you might want to include that information as well. You might also choose to note the name of the quilting teacher who inspired you or to tell a special story connected to the quilt.

Use the label to record key information about your quilt.

You can make a simple label by drawing and writing on fabric with permanent fabric markers. (Stabilize the fabric first with freezer paper or interfacing.) For a more elaborate (and fun!) label, use photo-transfer techniques, the lettering system on your sewing machine, or an embroidery machine to embellish your label. You could even create your own distinctive signature or logo. Include patches, decals, buttons, ribbons, or lace. I often include leftover blocks to tie the quilt top to the back.

Parade

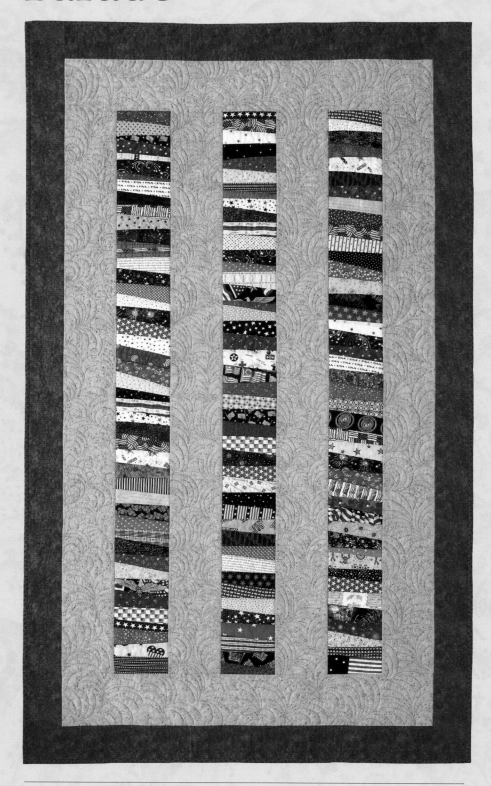

FREEDOM, PRIDE, AND COMMITMENT, designed and made by M'Liss Rae Hawley, machine quilted by Barbara Dau, 2007.

Finished quilt: 50½″ × 86½″

Finished pieced strip: 6″ × 66″

Here is the ultimate scrap quilt! You can make this one in no time using all kinds of bits and pieces. Strips can be sewn angled (like mine) or straight; they can vary in width; they can even be pieced! In fact, you can include leftover strata and segments from other strip-pieced projects, such as *Scrappy Kaleidoscope* (page 64), *Focus on a Theme* (page 29), and *Fence Rail* (page 55).

Whether you decide to go totally scrappy or choose prints that focus on a particular color scheme or theme, choose a fairly subtle fabric—one that won't compete with the pieced strips—for the alternate rows. I chose a gold batik with metallic stars to continue the patriotic theme. You may use a plain border or go with a more boldly printed fabric for the border.

I've also included an alternate size for this coins-style pattern. See page 26 for instructions on how to transform *Parade* into a decorative table runner.

materials

Yardage is based on 40"-wide fabric.

- 2¼ yards *total* of assorted prints for pieced strips
- 2 yards of fabric for alternate rows
- 2½ yards of fabric for outer border
- ⅞ yard of fabric for binding
- 5⅜ yards of fabric for backing
- ⅝ yard of fabric for hanging sleeve
- 59" × 95" piece of batting

cutting

Cut strips on the crosswise grain (from selvage to selvage) unless otherwise noted.

From the pieced-strip fabrics:

Cut a *total* of 120–150 strips, approximately 7" long and varying in width from 1¼" to 3".*

From the *lengthwise grain* of the alternate-row fabric:

Cut 4 strips, 6½" × 66½".

Cut 2 strips, 6½" × 42½".

From the *lengthwise grain* of the outer-border fabric:

Cut 2 strips, 4½" × 42½".**

Cut 2 strips, 4½" × 86½".**

From the binding fabric:

Cut 8 strips, 3" × 40".

From the hanging-sleeve fabric:

Cut 2 strips, 8½" × 40".

* This is an approximate number—enough to get you started. The exact number will depend on the number of strips you need to complete each 6" × 66" pieced strip. Cut additional strips as needed.

** Measure your quilt top before cutting. Refer to Squared Borders (page 14).

making the pieced strips

1. Cut a 6" × 66" piece of paper to use as a foundation. This can be craft paper, newsprint from a roll, butcher paper, or any paper of similar weight. If necessary, sew lengths of paper together to achieve the required measurement.

2. Determine an order for sewing your strips. Place the first strip right side up on one short end of the paper foundation. The short edges of the strip should slightly overlap the foundation. Stitch down the left edge of the strip with a ⅛"–³⁄₁₆" seam allowance.

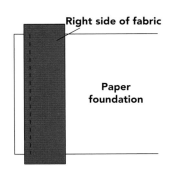

Right side of fabric

Paper foundation

ROLL IT UP!

3. Place the second strip over the first strip, right sides together and long raw edges aligned. Pin and sew using a scant $1/4''$ seam allowance. Open the second strip and press.

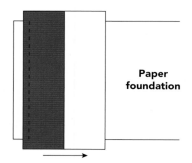

Paper foundation

4. Repeat Step 3 to sew the third strip, this time angling the strip slightly. Be sure that the stitching line includes a seam allowance of at least $1/4''$ of both fabrics for the entire length. Trim the seam allowance to $1/4''$.

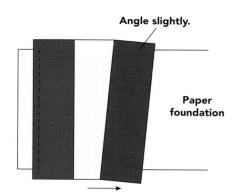

Angle slightly.

Paper foundation

5. Continue adding strips until the paper foundation is completely covered. Angle the strips slightly and change the direction of the angle every 2 or 3 strips. Trim the unit $1/4''$ beyond the foundation on all sides to measure $6^1/2'' \times 66^1/2''$.

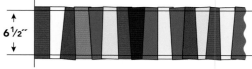

$6^1/2''$

6. Repeat Steps 1–5 to make a total of 3 pieced strips.

PARADE TIPS

- Use a dual-feed or walking foot for piecing (this is more important when working with heavier paper).

- When working with directional fabric (words, faces, motifs), take care to place it correctly—upside down to stitch.

- Bobby pins are another great way to hold both ends of the strips as you sew.

- Before you trim the strips, staystitch $1/8''$ from the edge of the paper to stabilize any bias edges.

- Consider stitching ribbons or trims and small embroidery motifs to the strips.

- When paper piecing, reduce the stitch length for easy paper removal.

assembling the quilt

1. Arrange the 3 pieced strips and the four $6\frac{1}{2}'' \times 66\frac{1}{2}''$ alternate-row strips, alternating them as shown in the assembly diagram. Sew the strips and rows. Press the seams toward the alternate-row strips.

2. Sew $6\frac{1}{2}'' \times 42\frac{1}{2}''$ alternate-row strips to the top and bottom of the quilt. Press the seams toward the alternate-row strips.

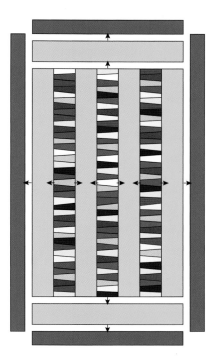

Quilt assembly diagram

3. Refer to Squared Borders (page 14). Measure, trim, and sew the outer-border strips to the top and bottom of the quilt. Press the seams toward the border. Repeat to sew the outer-border strips to the sides. Press.

finishing the quilt

Refer to Preparing Your Quilt for Quilting, Quilting Your Quilt, and Finishing Your Quilt (pages 16–21).

1. If you haven't already, carefully remove all paper foundations.

2. Piece the backing as described on page 17.

3. Layer the quilt top, batting, and backing; baste.

4. Hand or machine quilt as desired.

5. Use the 3''-wide strips to bind the edges of the quilt.

6. Add a hanging sleeve and label if desired.

CREATIVE OPTION

Rounded corners make a nice alternative for finishing your Parade quilt, as well as many other quilts in this book. You'll need to plan for rounded corners as soon as you begin making decisions about your borders—including your choice of quilting motifs—so you don't lose any important design elements.

No fancy tools are required. Just use an appropriately sized dinner plate to gently round the corners of your quilt as you prepare the quilted sandwich for binding. Add the serpentine stitch to the edges as usual (see page 19). Depending on the degree of the curve, you may need to cut binding strips from the bias of the fabric. However, test your fabric first, as many fabrics have enough give in the crosswise grain (selvage to selvage) to handle gentle curves. Whether you use bias or crosswise-cut strips, make sure you use lots of pins when sewing the binding around those curves.

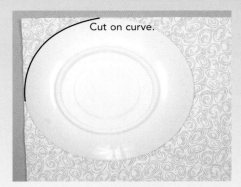

Cut on curve.

Parade: Version II

RAIN SHADOW WINES, pieced by Susie Kincy,
machine quilted by Barbara Dau, 2007.

Finished table runner: $20\frac{1}{2}'' \times 80\frac{1}{2}''$

Finished pieced strip: $6'' \times 66''$

he Parade unit, given its long, narrow shape, makes a great table runner, as you can see from this wonderful interpretation by Susie Kincy. To adapt the runner to fit your table, simply adjust the width and length of the paper foundation and the length of the individual strips accordingly.

materials

Yardage is based on 40″-wide fabric.

◆ 1 yard *total* of assorted prints for pieced strips

◆ 2 yards of fabric for alternate rows

◆ 2⅜ yards of fabric for outer border

◆ ⅝ yard of fabric for binding

◆ 2½ yards of fabric for backing

◆ 29″ × 89″ piece of batting

* Yardage is approximate. You may need more or less depending on the length and width of the strips you cut.

cutting

Cut strips on the crosswise grain (from selvage to selvage) unless otherwise noted.

From the pieced-strip fabrics:

Cut a total of 40–50 strips, approximately 7″ long and varying in width from 1¼″ to 3″.*

From the *lengthwise grain* of the alternate-row fabric:

Cut 2 strips, 3½″ × 66½″.

Cut 2 strips, 3½″ × 12½″.

From the *lengthwise grain* of the outer-border fabric:

Cut 2 strips, 4½″ × 12½″.**

Cut 2 strips, 4½″ × 80½″.**

From the binding fabric:

Cut 6 strips, 3″ × 40″.

* This is an approximate number—enough to get you started. The exact number will depend on the number of strips you need to complete the pieced strip. Cut additional strips as needed.

** Measure your table runner before cutting. Refer to Squared Borders (page 14).

making the table runner

1. Make 1 pieced strip, following the instructions in Making the Pieced Strips, Steps 1–5 (pages 23–24).

2. Sew a 3½″ × 66½″ alternate-row strip to opposite sides of the pieced strip from Step 1, as shown in the table runner assembly diagram. Press the seams toward the alternate-row strips.

3. Sew 3½″ × 12½″ alternate-row strips to the top and bottom of the table runner. Press the seams toward the strips.

4. Refer to Squared Borders (page 14). Measure, trim, and sew the outer-border strips to the top and bottom of the quilt. Press the seams toward the border. Repeat to sew the outer-border strips to the sides. Press.

5. Finish the table runner as described in Preparing Your Quilt for Quilting, Quilting Your Quilt, and Finishing Your Quilt (pages 16–21).

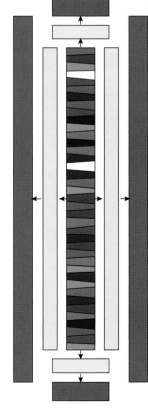

Table runner assembly diagram

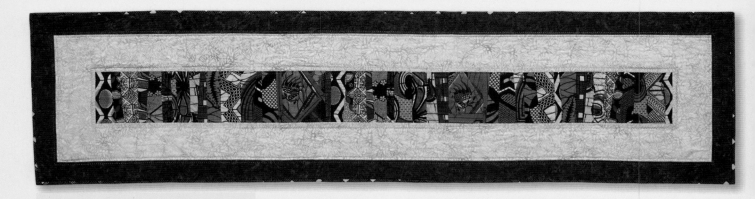

TABLES IN AFRICA,
80″ × 20″.

*Pieced and hand quilted
by Lucia Pan, 2007.*

DOWN THE HOSTA HIGHWAY,
50½″ × 86½″.

*Pieced by John James, machine quilted
by Barbara Dau, 2007.*

AFRICAN PARADE—BRIGHT AND BEAUTIFUL,
50″ × 86″.

*Pieced by Carla Zimmermann, machine
quilted by Kim McKinnon, 2007.*

Focus on a Theme

ELEMENTS OF STYLE, designed and made by M'Liss Rae Hawley, machine quilted by Barbara Dau, 2006.

Finished quilt: 57½˝ × 67½˝

Finished block: 10˝ × 10˝

C hoosing a theme—and then selecting an array of fabrics to reflect that theme—is one of my favorite ways of working. For this quilt, I decided on an Asian theme, chose as my focus fabric a large-scale print fabric from my Kimono Arts II line, and paired that fabric with a wide range of colorful, complementary batiks to establish my scrappy palette. It works well with my Quilting with M'Liss embroidery collection.

This block is incredibly easy to piece. Its large open field is ideal for featuring theme-related embroidery, appliqué, photo transfers, specialty fabrics, elaborate quilting motifs, or any combination of these possibilities. You'll find a variety of examples in the Creative Options box (page 33) and in the gallery for this chapter, beginning on page 34.

I cut two strips from each of the seventeen strip-set fabrics and made strata in identical pairs. If you prefer, you can use one 1½″-wide strip each of 34 different fabrics for a totally scrappy result. Either way, the outcome is fabulous!

materials

Yardage is based on 40″-wide fabric.

- 2½ yards of fabric for embroidered square backgrounds
- ¼ yard each of 17 fabrics for strip sets
- ⅓ yard of fabric for inner border
- 1½ yards of fabric for outer border
- ⅔ yard of fabric for binding
- 4⅜ yards of fabric for backing
- ⅝ yard of fabric for hanging sleeve
- 66″ × 76″ piece of batting
- 6 yards of 12″-wide stabilizer
- Embroidery threads in assorted colors

cutting

Cut strips on the crosswise grain (from selvage to selvage).

From the background fabric:

Cut 7 strips, 10½″ × 40″. Crosscut into 20 rectangles, 10½″ × 12″.*

From each strip-set fabric:

Cut 2 strips, 1½″ × 40″ (34 total).

From the inner-border fabric:

Cut 5 strips, 1½″ × 40″.

From the outer-border fabric:

Cut 6 strips, 8″ × 40″.

From the binding fabric:

Cut 7 strips, 3″ × 40″.

From the hanging-sleeve fabric:

Cut 2 strips, 8½″ × 40″.

* *Adjust size as needed to fit your embroidery hoop.*

PLAN AHEAD!

Whenever I purchase new fabric, I immediately launder and press it. Before folding it and placing it on the shelf, I cut off a 1½″-wide strip. When I want to make a scrappy quilt, such as this one, or a Fence Rail or Log Cabin, the strips are already cut!

making the blocks

Before beginning the embroidery, test the stabilizer with your background fabric to make sure the two are compatible. Make sure to use enough stabilizer to keep the embroidery flat throughout the stitching process. Refer to Tips for Machine Embroidery (page 42) for additional guidance.

1. Follow the manufacturer's directions to stabilize each $10^{1}/_{2}$″ × 12″ background rectangle. In each rectangle, center and embroider a favorite motif that fits in a 7″ × 7″ square. Trim each embroidered rectangle to $7^{1}/_{2}$″ × $7^{1}/_{2}$″. Make 20.

Make 20 of various motifs.

PERFECT PRESSING!

After you take the embroidery out of the hoop, press the embroidered piece right side down on a terry towel; then trim to the required size.

2. Arrange and sew together 7 assorted $1^{1}/_{2}$″ × 40″ strips to make a strip set. Press. Make 2 strip sets. Cut a total of 20 segments, each $3^{1}/_{2}$″ wide, from the strip sets.

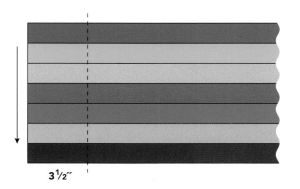

$3^{1}/_{2}$″

Make 2 strip sets. Cut 20 segments.

3. Arrange and sew together 10 assorted $1^{1}/_{2}$″ × 40″ strips to make a strip set. Press. Make 2 strip sets. Cut a total of 20 segments, each $3^{1}/_{2}$″ wide, from the strip sets.

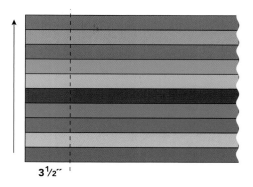

$3^{1}/_{2}$″

Make 2 strip sets. Cut 20 segments.

4. Sew a segment from Step 2 to the bottom edge of a $7^{1}/_{2}$″ embroidered square from Step 1. Press. Sew a segment from Step 3 to the left edge. Press. Make 6 and label them Block 1.

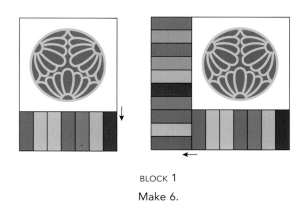

BLOCK 1

Make 6.

5. Sew a segment from Step 2 to the right edge of a $7^{1}/_{2}$″ embroidered square from Step 1. Press. Sew a segment from Step 3 to the bottom edge. Press. Make 4 and label them Block 2.

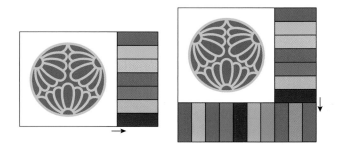

BLOCK 2

Make 4.

6. Sew a segment from Step 2 to the left edge of a 7½˝ embroidered square from Step 1. Press. Sew a segment from Step 3 to the top edge. Press. Make 6 and label them Block 3.

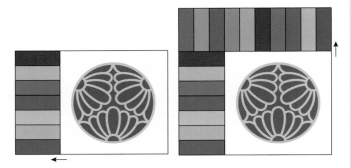

BLOCK 3

Make 6.

7. Sew a segment from Step 2 to the top edge of a 7½˝ embroidered square from Step 1. Press. Sew a segment from Step 3 to the right edge. Press. Make 4 and label them Block 4.

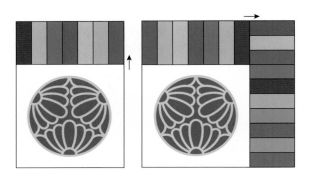

BLOCK 4

Make 4.

assembling the quilt

1. Arrange the blocks in 5 horizontal rows of 4 blocks each, as shown in the assembly diagram. Sew the blocks together into rows. Press the seams in alternating directions from row to row. Sew the rows together. Press.

Assembly diagram

2. Refer to Squared Borders (page 14). Measure, trim, and sew 1½˝-wide inner-border strips to the top, bottom, and sides of the quilt, piecing the strips as necessary. Press the seams toward the border.

3. Repeat Step 2 to measure, trim, and sew the 8˝-wide outer-border strips to the quilt, piecing the strips as necessary. Press the seams toward the outer border.

finishing the quilt

Refer to Preparing Your Quilt for Quilting, Quilting Your Quilt, and Finishing Your Quilt (pages 16–21).

1. Piece the backing as described on page 17.

2. Layer the quilt top, batting, and backing; baste.

3. Hand or machine quilt as desired.

4. Use the 3˝-wide strips to bind the edges of the quilt.

5. Add a hanging sleeve and label if desired.

CREATIVE OPTIONS

Here are just a few clever alternatives to substitute for theme-related machine embroidery in the open area of the Focus on a Theme block.

John James appliquéd a variety of military patches to the squares in the quilt he made to commemorate his service in the Marine Corps. To accommodate additional patches, he incorporated cornerstones in the outer border. See page 34 for a full view of John's quilt.

The large square in this block makes a suitably sized showcase for a selection of large-scale or other theme-related fabrics. Susie Kincy cut her squares from a variety of fabrics that reflect her quilt's "loving" theme. She embroidered others to continue the wedding anniversary theme. Her full quilt appears on page 35.

Detail of *Twenty Years*

Detail of *22 Years in the USMC*

To enhance her ethnic theme, Lucia Pan cut circles from various African fabrics and hand appliquéd them to the large squares. See page 36 for a full view of her quilt.

Carla Zimmermann used a collection of theme-related batik panels for her underwater quilt (see page 37 for the full quilt). If your pieces of specialty fabric are smaller than the required 7½˝ measurement, enlarge them with filler strips to fit the space.

Detail of *Circles from Africa*

Detail of *San Juan Undersea Garden*

22 YEARS IN THE USMC,
56″ × 65″.

*Pieced and appliquéd by John James,
machine quilted by Barbara Dau, 2006.*

TWENTY YEARS,
42″ × 52″.

*Pieced and embroidered by Susie Kincy,
machine quilted by Barbara Dau, 2007.*

CIRCLES FROM AFRICA,
54″ × 64″.

*Pieced, appliquéd, and hand quilted
by Lucia Pan, 2007.*

SAN JUAN UNDERSEA GARDEN,
58″ × 68″.

*Pieced by Carla Zimmermann, machine
quilted by Arlene Anderson, 2007.*

Embroidered Expressions

COI DRAGON, designed and made by M'Liss Rae Hawley, machine quilted by Barbara Dau, 2006.

Finished quilt: 33½˝ × 41½˝

Finished block: 8˝ × 8˝

've been embroidering in one form or another ever since I was four years old, so I guess it's just natural that I would include embroidery in my books.

Coi Dragon was originally designed to showcase the embroidery motifs, but it also makes a great scrap quilt. The simple block creates a subtle interplay of color and value and accommodates any theme. Have fun selecting fabrics to complement the embroideries, all from my Kimono Art collection.

For my quilt, I used the same red tonal Kimono Art fabric to surround the embroideries throughout the quilt. For a scrappier version, you can use a different fabric for each block.

materials

Yardage is based on 40″-wide fabric. For the fabrics framing the embroideries (Fabrics A and B), I recommend that you select fabrics with random, overall patterns rather than one-way, directional prints.

- ⅞ yard of fabric for embroidered square backgrounds
- ⅜ yard of fabric for embroidery "frames" (Fabric A)
- ⅛ yard each of 12 assorted fabrics for embroidery "frames" (Fabric B)
- ¼ yard of fabric for inner border
- ¾ yard of fabric for outer border
- ½ yard of fabric for binding
- 1½ yards of fabric for backing
- ⅜ yard of fabric for hanging sleeve
- 42″ × 50″ piece of batting
- 3¼ yards of 12″-wide stabilizer
- Embroidery threads in assorted colors

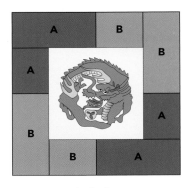

Block diagram
A and B denote Fabrics A and B.

cutting

Cut strips on the crosswise grain (from selvage to selvage).

From the embroidered-square background fabric:

Cut 3 strips, 9½″ × 40″. Crosscut into 12 squares, 9½″ × 9½″.*

From the ½ yard of embroidery-"frames" fabric (Fabric A):

Cut 5 strips, 2¼″ × 40″. Crosscut into:

    24 pieces, 2¼″ × 2¾″, and

    24 pieces, 2¼″ × 4½″.

From each of the 12 assorted embroidery-"frames" fabrics (Fabric B):

Cut 1 strip 2¼″ × 40″. Crosscut into:

    2 pieces, 2¼″ × 2¾″, and

    2 pieces, 2¼″ × 4½″.

From the inner-border fabric:

Cut 4 strips, 1″ × 40″.

From the outer-border fabric:

Cut 5 strips, 4½″ × 40″.

From the binding fabric:

Cut 5 strips, 3″ × 40″.

From the hanging-sleeve fabric:

Cut 1 strip, 8½″ × 40″.

* *Adjust as needed to fit your embroidery hoop.*

making the blocks

1. Follow the manufacturer's directions to stabilize each 9½″ background square. Center and embroider a favorite motif in each square. Trim each embroidered square to 5″ × 5″.

2. With right sides together, sew together a 2¼″ × 2¾″ Fabric A piece and a 2¼″ × 4½″ Fabric B piece, as shown. Press. Make 2 matching units.

Make 2.

3. Using the same Fabric B and with right sides together, sew together a 2¼″ × 4½″ Fabric A piece and a 2¼″ × 2¾″ Fabric B piece. Press. Make 2 matching units.

Make 2.

4. With right sides together and the top edges aligned, sew a unit from Step 2 to the left edge of an embroidered square. Stop stitching approximately 2″ from the square's bottom corner.

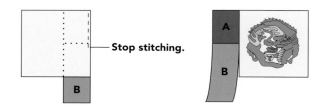

Stop stitching.

5. Align and sew a unit from Step 3 to the square's top edge. (This time you will sew the complete seam.) Press the seams toward the newly added unit.

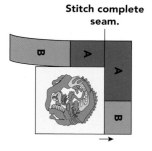

Stitch complete seam.

6. Align and sew the remaining unit from Step 2 to the square's right edge. Press.

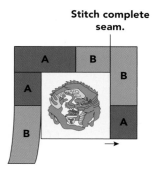

Stitch complete seam.

7. Sew the remaining unit from Step 3 to the block's bottom edge. Press.

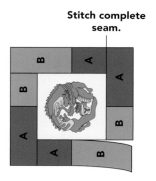

Stitch complete seam.

8. Complete the first seam (Step 4) and press.

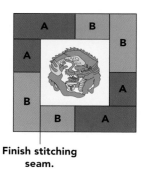

Finish stitching seam.

9. Repeat Steps 2–8 to make a total of 12 blocks.

assembling the quilt

10. Arrange the blocks in 4 horizontal rows of 3 blocks each, as shown in the assembly diagram. Sew the blocks into rows. Press the seams in alternating directions from row to row. Sew the rows together; press.

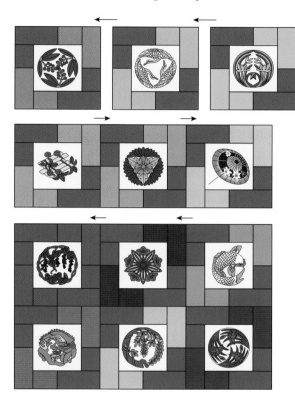

Assembly diagram

11. Refer to Squared Borders (page 14). Measure, trim, and sew 1″-wide inner-border strips to the top and bottom of the quilt. Press the seams toward the border. Repeat to sew the remaining 1″-wide inner-border strips to the sides. Press.

12. Repeat Step 2 to measure, trim, and sew the 4½″-wide outer-border strips to the quilt, piecing the strips as necessary. Press the seams toward the outer border.

finishing the quilt

Refer to Preparing Your Quilt for Quilting, Quilting Your Quilt, and Finishing Your Quilt (pages 16–21).

13. Layer the quilt top, batting, and backing; baste.

14. Hand or machine quilt as desired.

15. Use the 3″-wide strips to bind the edges of the quilt.

16. Add a hanging sleeve and label if desired.

MAKE THEM POP!

Want your embroideries to pop? Stipple quilt the background fabric in each embroidered square. Don't forget to stitch inside the motifs as well.

Tips for Machine Embroidery

The Embroidered Expressions quilt includes blocks that feature machine embroidery and instructions for the *Focus on a Theme* quilt (page 29). In addition, various Creative Options throughout the book suggest ways to incorporate this technique. Here are some tips to help you get the best possible results.

- Prewash the fabric you plan to use as background for the embroidery designs. Washing will preshrink the fabric—a necessary step.

- Begin your embroidery with a new needle and change it during the process if the point becomes dull. Skipped stitches are one indication of a dull needle. A dull needle can also distort the design. Some embroidery designs have more than 10,000 stitches, so change the needle often.

- Outfit your machine with an embroidery foot.

- When you take the embroidery out of the hoop, clip all the threads—front and back.

- When pressing, place the embroidery upside down on a terry towel and press the background fabric. You may need to use spray starch or sizing.

- Prewind several bobbins with polyester, rayon, or cotton bobbin-fill thread, such as Robison-Anton filament polyester bobbin thread. Or purchase prewound bobbins, such as those manufactured by Robison-Anton. Choose white or black, using the background fabric as your guide. Or you may want to change the bobbin thread as the color of the top thread changes.

- Select a fabric stabilizer to use under the background fabric. Of the many types of stabilizers available, my favorite is a midweight tear-away product manufactured by Sulky (see Resources on page 94). Whichever you choose, read the manufacturer's instructions carefully. Some stabilizers are heat- or water-sensitive. I prefer a tear-away stabilizer when I machine embroider on 100% cotton fabric. If the fabric is prone to puckering, try a water-soluble or heat-sensitive stabilizer.

- An embroidery hoop is key, as it keeps the fabric from shifting as you embroider the designs. If possible, place the fabric in the hoop so that it is on the straight grain. Avoid puckers and pleats. The fabric should be pulled taut but not too tight.

- Stitch a test of the desired embroidery design, using the fabric, threads, and stabilizer you plan to use for the project. You'll be able to tell whether the thread tension is correct, whether the thread coverage is sufficient, and whether the embroidered design will look good on the background fabric you've chosen so you can make any necessary adjustments. If you wish, you can incorporate your test design into your label or quilt backing.

MARDI GRAS,
33½″ × 41½″.

Designed and made by M'Liss Rae Hawley,
machine quilted by Barbara Dau, 2007.

WHEN I'M AWAY, MY BEARS PLAY,
33″ × 41″.

*Pieced and embroidered by
Annette Barca, machine quilted by
Barbara Dau, 2007.*

LANTERN MEDLEY,
33″ × 41″.

*Pieced and embroidered by
Anastasia Riordan, machine quilted
by Barbara Dau, 2007.*

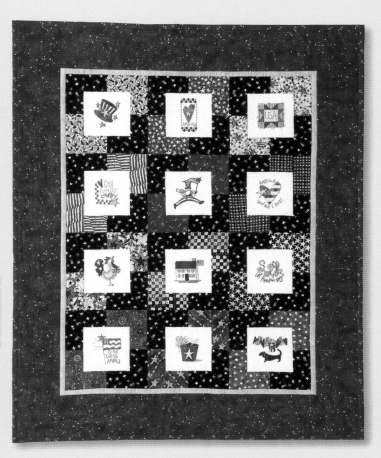

CELEBRATE AMERICA,
33″ × 41″.

*Pieced and embroidered by
Susie Kincy, machine quilted by
Barbara Dau, 2007.*

ECO ETHNO,
32½″ × 40″.

*Pieced by John James,
machine quilted by Barbara Dau, 2007.*

Shooting Star

IN THE LIMELIGHT, designed and made by M'Liss Rae Hawley, machine quilted by Barbara Dau, 2006.

Finished quilt: 33¼" × 40¾"

Finished block: 7½" × 7½"

I do a great deal of my sewing at night and enjoy taking a break now and then to look at the stars. I see them as sparks of color glittering in the inky black sky.

To capture this look in my quilt, I chose a single black batik for the block backgrounds and a variety of chartreuse batiks—suggested by the border fabric, which I planned to use all along—for star centers. Beyond that, my choices were much more random: I just selected two different, colorful batiks for the star points in each block. I added couching in the border to suggest star trails, a detail that worked well to tie the quilt together, both creatively and thematically.

This is a wonderful quilt for a beginner. Although the blocks are set side by side, none of the points touch, which is unusual for a star block! For this reason, it also makes a great choice for a group quilt, where slight variations in block size can sometimes be a problem.

materials

Yardage is based on 40″-wide fabric.

- ²⁄₃ yard of fabric for block background (A and C)
- One 2″ × 2″ square *each* of 12 assorted prints for star centers (D)
- Two 3⁷⁄₈″ × 3⁷⁄₈″ squares *each* of 12 assorted prints for star points (B)
- One 4¼″ × 4¼″ square *each* of 12 assorted prints for star points (E)
- ¼ yard of fabric for inner border
- 1³⁄₈ yards of fabric for outer border and binding
- 1½ yards of fabric for backing
- ³⁄₈ yard of fabric for hanging sleeve
- 41″ × 49″ piece of batting
- Assorted decorative threads, ribbons, and yarns for couching

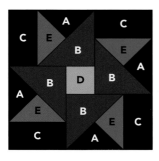

Block diagram

cutting

Cut strips on the crosswise grain (from selvage to selvage) unless otherwise noted.

From the background fabric:

Cut 2 strips, 4¼″ × 40″. Crosscut into 12 squares, 4¼″ × 4¼″. Cut each square in half twice diagonally to make 4 quarter-square triangles (48 total) (A).

Cut 5 strips, 2″ × 40″. Crosscut into 48 rectangles, 2″ × 3½″ (C).

From the assorted star point prints:

Cut each 3⁷⁄₈″ square in half once diagonally to make 2 half-square triangles (48 total) (B).

From the assorted star point prints:

Cut each 4¼″ square in half twice diagonally to make 4 quarter-square triangles (48 total) (E).

From the inner-border fabric:

Cut 4 strips, ⁷⁄₈″ × 40″.

From the lengthwise grain of the outer-border and binding fabric:

Cut 4 strips, 5″ × 46″.

Cut 4 strips, 3″ × 46″.

From the hanging-sleeve fabric:

Cut 1 strip, 8½″ × 40″.

making the blocks

1. With right sides together, sew one print quarter-square triangle (E) to one background quarter-square triangle (A) along one short edge, as shown. Press. Make 48 in matching sets of 4.

Make 48.

2. With right sides together, sew one print half-square triangle (B) to each unit from Step 1, as shown. Press. Make 48 in matching sets of 4.

Make 48.

3. With right sides together, sew one 2″ × 3½″ background rectangle (C) to each unit from Step 2, as shown. Press. Make 48.

Make 48.

4. Arrange one 2″ star center square and 4 matching units from Step 3, labeling the units as shown.

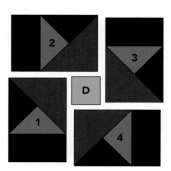

5. With right sides together, sew the star center square to the upper-right edge of Unit 1, stopping approximately halfway with a backstitch to make a partial seam. Finger-press the seam away from the square.

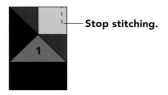

6. Sew the remaining units around the star center square in the order shown, rotating the block as you sew each seam. Press the seams away from the square.

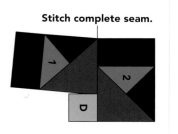

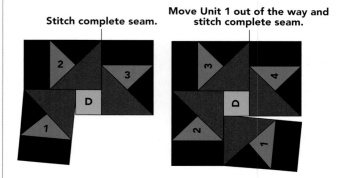

7. Finish sewing the seam between Unit 1 and the center square/Unit 4. Press the seam away from the square.

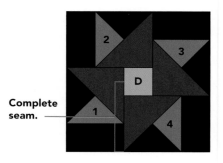

8. Repeat Steps 4–7 to complete 12 Shooting Star blocks.

FUSSY CUT FOR FUN!

If your quilt is built around a specific theme, you might like to choose a fabric (or fabrics) with motifs you can fussy cut for the star centers (piece D), as Annette Barca did for her quilt *Happy Dog Days with Matilda*, in honor of Adrienne's beloved dachshund.

Detail of a Shooting Star block with fussy-cut center from Annette Barca's quilt.
For a full view of this quilt, see page 52.

assembling the quilt

1. Arrange the blocks in 4 horizontal rows of 3 blocks each, as shown in the assembly diagram.

2. Sew the blocks together into rows. Press. Sew the rows together. Press.

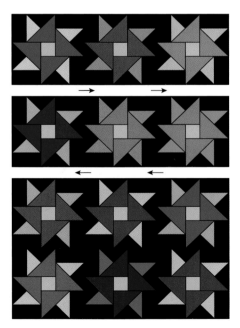

Assembly diagram

3. Refer to the Couching tip box on page 50 to couch a variety of decorative threads, ribbons, and yarns onto each 5″-wide outer-border strip.

4. Fold each ⅞″-wide inner-border strip in half lengthwise to find and mark its midpoint. Repeat with each embellished 5″-wide outer-border strip. With right sides together, midpoints matched, and long raw edges aligned, sew the inner-border strips to the embellished outer-border strips in pairs, as shown. Press. Make 4.

Midpoint

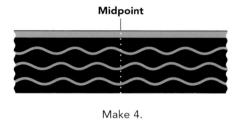

Make 4.

5. Refer to Mitered Borders (page 15) to measure, fit, and sew the border units to the quilt. Miter the corners. Press the seams toward the border units.

WHO SAYS . . .

. . . a quilt must have square corners? Take a look at *Beach Beauties under the Northwest Sun* (page 53). Carla Zimmermann's clever border treatment makes good use of the beach cottage border print.

finishing the quilt

Refer to Preparing Your Quilt for Quilting, Quilting Your Quilt, and Finishing Your Quilt (pages 16-21).

1. Layer the quilt top, batting, and backing; baste.

2. Hand or machine quilt as desired.

3. Use the 3″-wide strips to bind the edges of the quilt.

4. Add a hanging sleeve and label if desired.

COUCHING

I love to add couching to my quilts. It creates visual interest and texture, while at the same time allowing me to enhance the theme of my quilt with an additional layer of creativity.

Couching is an embellishment technique that involves using decorative topstitching to attach a variety of decorative threads, yarns, or ribbons to the surface of a quilt. Here are some tips for a creative—and successful—couching experience:

♦ Experiment first! Select a variety of trims and threads that complement your fabric choices and quilt theme. The more you have to choose from, the better! Couch the threads and trims to a sample of the intended background fabric, using a variety of stitches in both matching and contrasting threads. This allows you to discover what works best for your quilt and which foot works best for each trim and stitch. Document your findings for easy reference.

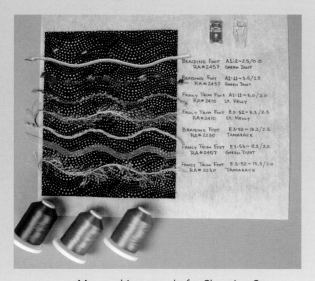

My couching sample for Shooting Stars

♦ Cut the outer border as instructed. Then cut a strip of tear-away stabilizer 1″ wider than the border width × the border length. Use a spray adhesive or pins to secure the stabilizer to the wrong side of the border strip.

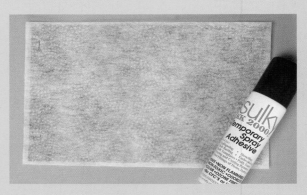

♦ Allowing for a ¼″ seam allowance, use a chalk marker to draw three serpentine (curvy) lines on the right side of the stabilized border strip. Space the lines somewhat evenly, but don't worry about the corners. As you see in the quilt photo on page 46 and in the corner detail below, they don't need to match to look good.

♦ Referring to your couching sample and working one line at a time, place your selected yarns and threads over the marked lines and stitch the trims in place. Remove the stabilizer and sew the borders to the quilt as instructed.

Detail of couching on *In the Limelight* (page 46): I used three different trims on each side of my quilt and stitched them in place with color-matched thread.

AUTUMN STARS,
32½˝ × 39½˝.

Pieced by John and Louise James,
machine quilted by Barbara Dau, 2007.

HAPPY DOG DAYS WITH MATILDA,
31″ × 40″.

Pieced and embroidered by Annette Barca, machine quilted by Barbara Dau, 2007.

STAR PINWHEEL,
32½″ × 41″.

Pieced by Leslie Rommann, machine quilted by Peggy Wilbur, 2007.

*Pieced by Carla Zimmermann,
machine quilted by Arlene Anderson, 2007.*

*Pieced by Susie Kincy, machine
quilted by Barbara Dau, 2007.*

PRIMARY PINWHEELS,
33½″ × 40½″.

Pieced by Marie Miller, machine quilted by Barbara Dau, 2007.

FUNKY 4TH OF JULY,
33″ × 40″.

Pieced by Anastasia Riordan, machine quilted by Barbara Dau, 2007.

Fence Rail

I LOVE LIFE!, designed and made by M'Liss Rae Hawley,
machine quilted by Barbara Dau, 2007.

Finished quilt: 50$\frac{1}{2}$˝ × 64$\frac{1}{2}$˝

Finished block: 7˝ × 7˝

One of my favorite sewing pastimes is sewing strips of fabric together to create blocks and strata. So, the Fence Rail block is a natural for me. What a great way to use those 1½″-wide strips of fabric I keep handy (see page 7)! In fact, the Fence Rail makes such a perfect scrap quilt—and is *so* easy to sew—that I've included two different-sized options for you: a lap quilt/twin-bed comforter size and a smaller version, well-suited for a wall or crib, made by Marie Miller (page 59).

I used 1½″-wide strips of 175 different batiks in my version of the Fence Rail. When you include the collection of pinks (one of my color favorites) that I used for the blocks' corner triangles, the fabric total climbs to more than 200. That's quite a treasury of fabrics.

I finished off the outer border on my quilt by machine embroidering colorful floral motifs from my Kimono Art II embroidery collection. The floral sprays turn two opposite corners. You'll find additional border ideas in the Creative Options box (page 58) and in the fabulous gallery of quilts for this chapter, beginning on page 61.

materials

Yardage is based on 40″-wide fabric.

- 1⅜ yards *total* of assorted colorful prints for blocks (A)
- 1¼ yards *total* of assorted prints in a single color for blocks (B)
- ⅓ yard of fabric for inner border
- 1⅜ yards of fabric for outer border
- ⅔ yard of fabric for binding
- 4⅛ yards of fabric for backing
- ⅝ yard of fabric for hanging sleeve
- 59″ × 73″ piece of batting
- 3½ yards 12″-wide stabilizer for embroidered borders (optional)
- Embroidery threads in assorted colors for embroidered borders (optional)

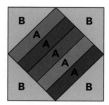

Block diagram

cutting

Cut strips on the crosswise grain (from selvage to selvage).

From the assorted colorful prints:

Cut a *total* of 175 strips, 1½″ × 6½″ (A).

From the assorted prints in a single color:

Cut a *total* of 70 squares, 4½″ × 4½″. Cut each square in half once diagonally to make 2 half-square triangles (140 total) (B).

From the inner-border fabric:

Cut 5 strips, 1½″ × 40″.

From the outer-border fabric:

Cut 6 strips, 7″ × 40″.

From the binding fabric:

Cut 7 strips, 3″ × 40″.

From the hanging-sleeve fabric:

Cut 2 strips, 8½″ × 40″.

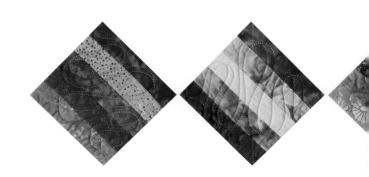

making the blocks

1. Arrange 5 assorted $1\frac{1}{2}'' \times 6\frac{1}{2}''$ strips in a pleasing visual order. With right sides together and long raw edges aligned, sew the strips together. Press. Square up the units to measure $5\frac{1}{2}'' \times 5\frac{1}{2}''$. Make 35.

Make 35.

2. Sew assorted half-square triangles to opposite sides of each unit from Step 1. Press. Sew assorted half-square triangles to the remaining sides. Press. Square up the blocks to measure $7\frac{1}{2}''$, taking care to leave a $\frac{1}{4}''$ seam allowance all around. Make 35 blocks.

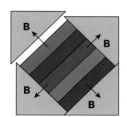

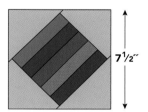

$7\frac{1}{2}''$

Make 35.

assembling the quilt

1. Arrange the blocks in 7 horizontal rows of 5 blocks each, alternating the orientation of the blocks from row to row, as shown in the assembly diagram. Sew the blocks together into rows. Press the seams in alternating directions from row to row. Sew the rows together. Press.

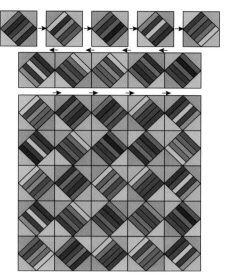

Lap quilt/twin-bed comforter assembly diagram

2. Refer to Squared Borders (page 14). Measure, trim, and sew $1\frac{1}{2}''$-wide inner-border strips to the top and bottom of the quilt. Press the seams toward the border. Repeat to sew $1\frac{1}{2}''$-wide inner-border strips to the sides, piecing the strips as necessary. Press.

3. Measure and trim a $7''$ outer-border strip to the top and bottom of the quilt. Press the seams toward the outer border. Repeat to sew $7''$-wide outer-border strips to the sides, piecing the strips as necessary. Press.

finishing the quilt

Refer to Preparing Your Quilt for Quilting, Quilting Your Quilt, and Finishing Your Quilt (pages 16–21).

1. Piece the backing as described on page 17.

2. Layer the quilt top, batting, and backing; baste.

3. Hand or machine quilt as desired.

4. Use the $3''$-wide strips to bind the edges of the quilt.

5. Add a hanging sleeve and label if desired.

CREATIVE OPTIONS

If you wish, you can add embroidery to the outer-border strips as I did. Be sure to prepare the strips with stabilizer before you begin. Refer to Tips for Machine Embroidery (page 42) for additional guidance as needed.

Detail of embroidered border on *I Love Life!*

Here are a few additional ideas for creative border treatments.

Susie Kincy incorporated cornerstones into the outer borders of her Fence Rail quilt. She brewed up a theme-related touch by adding teapot embroideries to the corner squares in her quilt (see page 63 for the full quilt).

Detail of border on *Harmonious Blend*

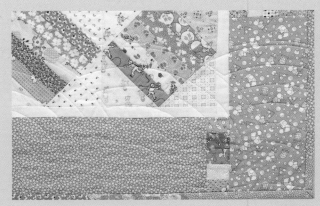

Detail of outer border of Annette's *Remembering the Past*

Leftover strips were put to good use by both Annette Barca (page 63) and Carla Zimmermann (page 62). Annette inserted slices of strata between segments of an outer border pieced from different 1930s green prints. Carla used extra strips to create a strip-pieced middle border for her version of the smaller wall/crib quilt.

Detail of pieced middle border of Carla's *Kansas Wheat around the Old Fence*

Fence Rail: Version II

PLAYTIME, NOT NAPTIME, *pieced by Marie Miller, machine quilted by Barbara Dau, 2007.*

Finished quilt: $46\frac{1}{2} \times 39\frac{1}{2}''$

Finished block: $7'' \times 7''$

arie Miller created a charming version of the Fence Rail quilt in an alternative, smaller size. This four-block by five-block version features a variety of purple prints, textures, and tonals, sure to appeal to any little one. Of course, you can make your quilt in any fabrics you choose.

materials

Yardage is based on 40″-wide fabric.

◆ 1 yard *total* of assorted prints for blocks (A)

◆ ¾ yard *total* of assorted prints in a single color for blocks (B)

◆ ¼ yard of fabric for inner border

◆ ⅞ yard of fabric for outer border

◆ ⅝ yard of fabric for binding

◆ 3¼ yards of fabric for backing

◆ ⅜ yard of fabric for hanging sleeve

◆ 48″ × 55″ piece of batting

cutting

Cut strips on the crosswise grain (from selvage to selvage).

From the assorted prints:

Cut a *total* of 100 strips, 1½″ × 6½″ (A).

From the assorted prints in a single color:

Cut a *total* of 40 squares, 4½″ × 4½″. Cut each square in half once diagonally to make 2 half-square triangles (80 total) (B).

From the inner-border fabric:

Cut 4 strips, 1½″ × 40″.

From the outer-border fabric:

Cut 5 strips, 5″ × 40″.

From the binding fabric:

Cut 5 strips, 3″ × 40″.

From the hanging-sleeve fabric:

Cut 2 strips, 8½″ × 40″.

making the wall/crib quilt

1. Follow the instructions in Making the Blocks for the larger quilt (page 57). Make 20 blocks.

2. Arrange the blocks in 4 horizontal rows of 5 blocks each, orienting them as shown in the assembly diagram. Sew the blocks together into rows. Press the seams in alternating directions from row to row. Sew the rows together. Press.

3. Refer to Squared Borders (page 14). Measure, trim, and sew 1½″-wide inner-border strips to the top and bottom of the quilt. Press the seams toward the border. Repeat to sew 1½″-wide inner-border strips to the sides.

4. Measure, trim, and sew 5″ outer-border strips to the top and bottom of the quilt. Press the seams toward the new border. Repeat to sew 5″-wide outer-border strips to the sides, piecing as necessary. Press.

5. Finish the quilt as described in Preparing Your Quilt for Quilting, Quilting Your Quilt, and Finishing Your Quilt (pages 16–21).

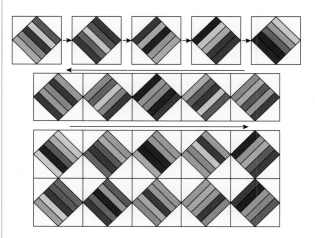

Wall/crib quilt assembly diagram

PURPLE PASSION,
38½″ × 45″.

Pieced by Anastasia Riordan,
machine quilted by Barbara Dau, 2007.

TREES OUT MY WINDOW,
38½″ × 63″.

*Pieced and machine quilted
by Barbara Dau, 2007.*

KANSAS WHEAT AROUND THE OLD FENCE,
39″ × 46″.

*Pieced by Carla Zimmermann, machine
quilted by Arlene Anderson, 2007.*

AFRICAN FRIENDS,
38″ × 46″.

*Pieced and hand quilted
by Lucia Pan, 2007.*

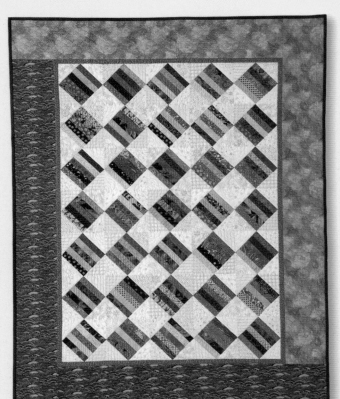

METALICA,
50″ × 64″.

*Pieced by John James,
machine quilted by Barbara Dau, 2007.*

REMEMBERING THE PAST,
47″ × 61″.

*Pieced by Annette Barca,
machine quilted by Barbara Dau, 2007.*

HARMONIOUS BLEND,
47″ × 61″.

*Pieced and embroidered by Susie Kincy,
machine quilted by Barbara Dau, 2007.*

Scrappy Kaleidoscope

THE MAGIC HOUR, designed and made by M'Liss Rae Hawley, machine quilted by Barbara Dau, 2007.

Finished quilt: 65½″ × 65½″

Finished block: 17″ × 17″

A Scrappy Kaleidoscope is the perfect quilt to start with: I think it is one of my favorite projects in this book, and it is also one of my favorite classes to teach. The quilt gives you a great canvas for revealing your fabric history. In my version, *The Magic Hour,* I included fabric from the first dress I ever made—in a Singer sewing class when I was just nine years old! My dad, ever supportive of my creative endeavors, fibbed about my age to get me into the class. (See page 5 for a detail of the quilt showing this cherished fabric.)

You can use leftover strips from loads of other projects to make these blocks. The quilt is also very fat quarter friendly. You can even use small amounts of corduroy, velvet, and cotton twills. I warn you, however—while it will make a dent in your scrap bag, you'll probably find, as you work on this quilt, that it is hard to resist adding more to your stash!

materials

Yardage is based on 40"-wide fabric.

- 4¼ yards *total* of a wide variety of prints, ranging in value from light to dark, for wedge strip sets (A)*

- ½ yard *total* of assorted light to light-medium prints for block corner triangles (B)**

- ½ yard *total* of assorted medium-dark to dark prints for block corner triangles (B)**

- ⅜ yard of fabric for inner border

- 1½ yards of fabric for outer border

- ¾ yard of fabric for binding

- 4¼ yards of fabric for backing

- ⅝ yard of fabric for hanging sleeve

- 74" × 74" piece of batting

- 9¼" kaleidoscope triangle ruler (optional)

* Yardage is approximate. You may need more or less depending on the widths of the strips you cut. Aim for a mix of about ⅓ light prints, ⅓ medium prints, and ⅓ dark prints.

** These may be the same color family—or not.

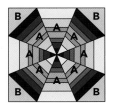

Block 1   Block 2

cutting

Cut strips on the crosswise grain (from selvage to selvage).

From the wide variety of prints ranging in value from light to dark (A):

Cut a *total* of 150 strips, 20" long and varying in width from 1¼" wide to 2½" wide.*

From the assorted light to light-medium prints for block corner triangles:

Cut a *total* of 8 squares, 5⅞" × 5⅞". Cut each square in half once diagonally to make 2 half-square triangles (16 total) (B).

From the assorted medium-dark to dark prints for block corner triangles:

Cut a *total* of 10 squares, 5⅞" × 5⅞". Cut each square in half once diagonally to make 2 half-square triangles (20 total) (B).

From the inner-border fabric:

Cut 6 strips, 1½" × 40".

From the outer-border fabric:

Cut 7 strips, 6½" × 40".

From the binding fabric:

Cut 7 strips, 3" × 40".

From the hanging-sleeve fabric:

Cut 2 strips, 8½" × 40".

* This is an approximate number. The exact number will depend on the number of strips you need to complete each 9½"-wide strata.

making the blocks

1. Sort the 20″-long assorted print strips by value (not by width) into lights, mediums, and darks.

2. Arrange 6–8 assorted strips of varying widths side by side from light to dark. When you are pleased with the arrangement, sew the strips together to make a strip set, as shown. You will want the strip set to finish at least 9½″ wide when the strips are sewn together. Press the seams toward the darker strips. Make 18 scrappy strip sets.

Make 18 strips sets.

STREAMLINE THE WORK!

For added efficiency, lay out and sew several strip sets at a time.

3. Use the pattern on page 68 to make a template for the wedge (A). As an option, you may use a kaleidoscope triangle ruler. Cut 4 wedges from each strip set by flipping the template as shown. You will have a total of 72 wedges, 36 with light at the bottom edge and 36 with dark at the bottom edge. As you cut, sort the wedges into 2 stacks: one with the lightest strip on the bottom edge ("light" wedges) and one with the darkest strip on the bottom edge ("dark" wedges).

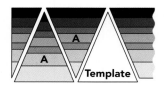

Cut 4 wedges from each strip set (72 total).

STRIP TIPS!

When you place the template or ruler on the strips, allow a *minimum* of ¾″ at the top and at the bottom. This leaves at least ½″ of fabric showing beyond the seams at the top and bottom of the triangle after the blocks are sewn together.

Vary the widths of the strata so they do not match when you sew the wedges together.

For the borders, depending on the variety of fabrics and the theme of your quilt, a plain or simple fabric may work best!

4. Arrange 4 light scrappy wedges and 4 dark scrappy wedges, alternating them as shown. I prefer to lay out the wedges for all 9 blocks before I begin sewing to make sure I have a good scrappy mix.

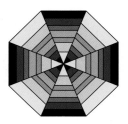

Arrange 8 wedges together.

5. Working one block at a time and with the light wedge on the bottom and the dark wedge on top, sew the wedges together in pairs. Press the seams toward the light wedges. Make 4 pairs for each block.

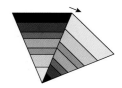

Make 4 pairs for each block.

OUTSIDE IN!

When sewing wedges together, stitch from the wide base of the wedge to the pointy center.

6. Sew 2 pairs from Step 5 together to complete each half of the unit. Press. Sew 2 half units together. Press.

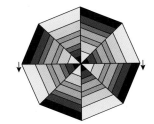

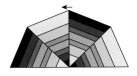

Make 2 half units for each block.

Make 9.

7. Repeat Steps 5 and 6 to make a total of 9 units.

8. Again working one block at a time, sew a medium-dark or dark print half-square triangle to the edge of each *light* wedge in the unit, as shown. Press. Make 5 and label them Block 1.

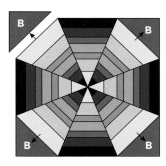

BLOCK 1
Make 5.

9. Sew a light or light-medium print half-square triangle to the edge of each *dark* wedge in each remaining unit as shown. Press. Make 4 and label them Block 2.

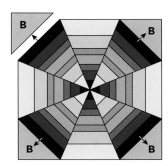

BLOCK 2
Make 4.

assembling the quilt

1. Arrange the blocks in 3 horizontal rows of 3 blocks each, alternating Blocks 1 and 2, as shown in the assembly diagram. Sew the blocks together into rows. Press the seams in alternating directions from row to row. Sew the rows together. Press.

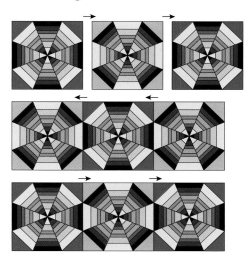

Assembly diagram

2. Refer to Squared Borders (page 14). Measure, trim, and sew 1½″-wide inner-border strips to the top and bottom of the quilt, piecing the strips as necessary. Press the seams toward the border. Repeat to sew the 1½″-wide inner-border strips to the sides of the quilt.

3. Repeat Step 2 to measure, trim, and sew the 6½″-wide outer-border strips to the quilt, piecing the strips as necessary. Press the seams toward the outer border.

finishing the quilt

Refer to Preparing Your Quilt for Quilting, Quilting Your Quilt, and Finishing Your Quilt (pages 16–21).

1. Piece the backing as described on page 17.

2. Layer the quilt top, batting, and backing; baste.

3. Hand or machine quilt as desired.

4. Use the 3″-wide strips to bind the edges of the quilt.

5. Add a hanging sleeve and label if desired.

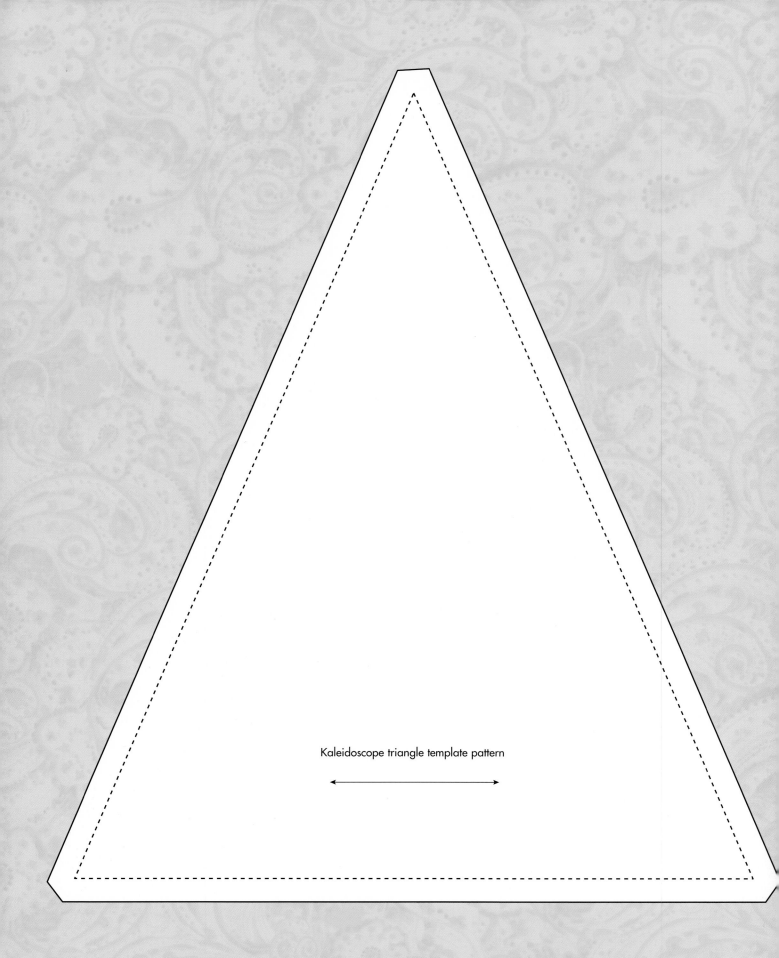

Kaleidoscope triangle template pattern

BRIGHT AND BOLD,
60˝ × 60˝.

Pieced by Annette Barca,
machine quilted by Barbara Dau, 2007.

HEARTS GALORE,
65˝ × 65˝.

Pieced by John and Louise James,
machine quilted by Barbara Dau, 2006.

VISIONS OF PROVENCE,
60″ × 77″.

Pieced by Marie Miller,
machine quilted by Barbara Dau, 2007.

KOWLOON KALEIDOSCOPE,
62″ × 62″.

*Pieced by Susie Kincy,
machine quilted by Barbara Dau, 2007.*

MY SCRAP BAG KALEIDOSCOPE,
62″ × 62″.

*Pieced by Vicki DeGraaf,
machine quilted by Stacie Johnson
and Debbie Webster, 2007.*

Gathering Moments

MY BIRTHDAY BASKETS, designed and made by M'Liss Rae Hawley, machine quilted by Barbara Dau, 2006.

Finished quilt: 39¼″ × 39¼″

Finished block: 10″ × 10″

athering Moments basket blocks are so popular with quilters, including scrap quilters, that I wanted to be sure to include one in this book. I decided to make my version a Christmas quilt because I've never made a Christmas quilt for any of my books. This seemed like a pretty big omission, given that Christmas Day is also my birthday!

To get started, I put all of my Christmas-themed fabrics in a stack and started pulling potential combinations. I settled on an on-point variation that would incorporate four different prints in each block: a light for the background, two different medium or dark prints for the small triangles, and a third medium or dark print for the basket itself.

I had so much fun making this little wall quilt that I decided to make a second, larger version (page 76) and give you the instructions for that one, too. Be sure to check out the Creative Options box (page 80) and the gallery of quilts for this chapter, beginning on page 81. You'll discover some terrific ideas, including a few for inventive embellishments!

materials

Yardage is based on 40″-wide fabric.

- ⅜ yard *each* of 4 light prints for block backgrounds (A, C, D)

- 4 squares 2⅞″ × 2⅞″ *each* of 4 assorted medium or dark print #1 for blocks (16 total) (A)

- 2 squares 2⅞″ × 2⅞″ *each* of 4 assorted medium or dark print #2 for blocks (8 total) (A)

- 1 square 2⅞″ × 2⅞″ (4 total) and 1 square 6⅞″ × 6⅞″ (4 total) *each* of 12 assorted medium or dark print #3 for blocks (A, B)

- 1¼ yards *total* of assorted light fabrics for setting square and setting triangles

- ¾ yard of fabric for outer border

- ⅝ yard of fabric for binding

- 2¾ yards of fabric for backing

- ⅜ yard of fabric for hanging sleeve

- 48″ × 48″ piece of batting

cutting

Cut strips on the crosswise grain (from selvage to selvage).

From *each* assorted background fabric:

Cut each 2⅞″ × 2⅞″ square in half once diagonally to make 2 half-square triangles (14 total) (A). (You will need 13 for each block—52 total for the quilt.)

Cut 2 strips, 2½″ × 6½″ (C). (You will need 2 for each block—8 total for the quilt.)

Cut the 4⅞″ × 4⅞″ square in half once diagonally to make 2 half-square triangles (D). (You will need 1 for each block—4 total for the quilt.)

From *each* assorted medium or dark print #1 fabric:

Cut each 2⅞″ × 2⅞″ square in half once diagonally to make 2 half-square triangles (8 total) (A). (You will need 7 for each block—28 total for the quilt.)

From *each* assorted medium or dark print #2 fabric:

Cut each 2⅞″ × 2⅞″ square in half once diagonally to make 2 half-square triangles (4 total) (A). (You will need 3 for each block—12 total for the quilt.)

From *each* assorted medium or dark print #3 fabric:

Cut each 2⅞″ × 2⅞″ square in half once diagonally to make 2 half-square triangles (2 total) (A). (You will need 2 for each block—8 total for the quilt.)

Cut the 6⅞″ × 6⅞″ square in half once diagonally to make 2 half-square triangles (2 total) (B). (You will need 1 for each block—4 total for the quilt.)

From the assorted setting-square and setting-triangle fabrics:

Cut 1 square, $10\frac{1}{2}'' \times 10\frac{1}{2}''$.

Cut 1 square, $17'' \times 17''$. Cut in half twice diagonally to make 4 quarter-square triangles.*

Cut 2 squares, $11'' \times 11''$. Cut each square in half once diagonally to make 2 half-square triangles (4 total).

From the outer-border fabric:

Cut 4 strips, $5'' \times 40''$.

From the binding fabric:

Cut 5 strips, $3'' \times 40''$.

From the hanging-sleeve fabric:

Cut 1 strip, $8\frac{1}{2}'' \times 40''$.

If you want the side-setting triangles to have a scrappier look, cut more than one $17'' \times 17''$ square into quarter-square triangles. You will then have several quarter-square triangles left over for future projects.

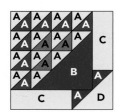

Block diagram

making the blocks

1. With right sides together, sew 1 half-square background triangle A and 1 half-square medium or dark print #1 triangle A together along the long edge. Press. Make 7 matching units.

Make 7.

2. Repeat Step 1 using the 2 matching medium or dark print #2 triangles. Make 3 matching units.

Make 3.

3. Arrange and sew together 4 units from Step 1, as shown. Press.

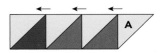

4. Arrange and sew together 1 matching half-square background triangle A, 2 units from Step 2, and 1 unit from Step 1, as shown. Press.

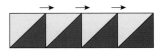

5. Arrange and sew together 1 matching half-square background triangle A and 1 unit *each* from Steps 1 and 2, as shown. Press.

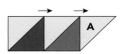

6. Arrange and sew together 1 matching half-square background triangle A and 1 unit from Step 1, as shown. Press.

7. Arrange and sew together the units from Steps 3–6, as shown. Press.

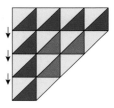

8. With right sides together, sew together 1 half-square medium or dark print #3 triangle B and the unit from Step 7, as shown. Press.

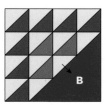

9. Cut the matching 2⅞″ medium or dark print #3 square in half once diagonally to make 2 half-square triangles. Sew together 1 half-square medium or dark print #3 triangle A and one 2½″ × 6½″ background rectangle C. Press. Make 1 of each.

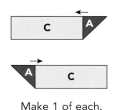

Make 1 of each.

10. Sew the units from Step 9 to adjacent sides of the unit from Step 8. Press.

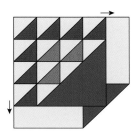

11. Sew a matching half-square background triangle D to the unit from Step 10. Press.

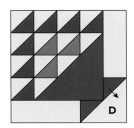

12. Repeat Steps 1–11 to make a total of 4 blocks.

assembling the quilt

The side and corner triangles are cut oversized so that the blocks appear to float. You will square up the quilt top after it is assembled.

1. Arrange the blocks, the 10½″ setting square, the quarter-square side-setting triangles, and the half-square corner-setting triangles in diagonal rows, as shown in the assembly diagram.

2. Sew the blocks, the setting square, and the side-setting triangles together into diagonal rows. Press the seams away from the Gathering Moments blocks.

3. Sew the rows together. Press. Trim the dog ears at each corner. Press the seams toward the triangles.

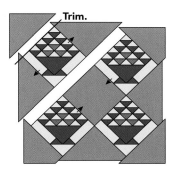

Small wall quilt assembly diagram

4. Square up the quilt top, measuring 1″ from the corners of the blocks to trim the side and corner triangles.

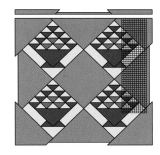

5. Refer to Squared Borders (page 14). Measure, trim, and sew 5″-wide outer-border strips to the top and bottom of the quilt. Press the seams toward the border. Repeat to sew the 5″-wide outer-border strips to the sides of the quilt.

finishing the quilt

Refer to Preparing Your Quilt for Quilting, Quilting Your Quilt, and Finishing Your Quilt (pages 16–21).

1. Piece the backing as described on page 17.

2. Layer the quilt top, batting, and backing; baste.

3. Hand or machine quilt as desired.

4. Use the 3″-wide strips to bind the edges of the quilt.

5. Add a hanging sleeve and label if desired.

Gathering Moments on Point: Version II

GATHERING LOVE, designed and made by M'Liss Rae Hawley, machine quilted by Barbara Dau, 2007.

Finished quilt: 56½″ × 70½″

Finished block: 10″ × 10″

I used the same fabric formula—one light and three different medium or dark prints—for each block in this larger version of the Gathering Moments quilt. I had fun pairing up my collection of white-with-black print backgrounds with the perky basket prints.

materials

Yardage is based on 40″-wide fabric.

- ³⁄₈ yard *each* of 12 assorted light prints for block backgrounds (A, C, D)

- 4 squares 2⁷⁄₈″ × 2⁷⁄₈″ *each* of 12 assorted medium or dark print #1 for blocks (48 total) (A)

- 2 squares 2⁷⁄₈″ × 2⁷⁄₈″ *each* of 12 assorted medium or dark print #2 for blocks (24 total) (A)

- 1 square 2⁷⁄₈″ × 2⁷⁄₈″ (12 total) and 1 square 6⁷⁄₈″ × 6⁷⁄₈″ (12 total) *each* of 12 assorted medium or dark print #3 for blocks (A, B)

- 1⁵⁄₈ yards *total* of assorted fabrics for setting squares and setting triangles

- ½ yard of fabric for inner border

- 1¼ yards of fabric for second and outer border

- ³⁄₈ yard of fabric for third border

- ¾ yard of fabric for binding

- 4½ yards of fabric for backing

- ⁵⁄₈ yard of fabric for hanging sleeve

- 65″ × 79″ piece of batting

cutting

Cut strips on the crosswise grain (from selvage to selvage).

From each assorted background fabric:

Cut 7 squares, 2⁷⁄₈″ × 2⁷⁄₈″. Cut each square in half once diagonally to make 2 half-square triangles (14 total) (A). (You will need 13 for each block—156 total for the quilt.)

Cut 2 strips, 2½″ × 6½″ (24 total) (C).

Cut 1 square, 4⁷⁄₈″ × 4⁷⁄₈″. Cut the square in half once diagonally to make 2 half-square triangles (D). (You will need 1 for each block—12 total for the quilt.)

From *each* assorted medium or dark print #1 fabric:

Cut each 2⁷⁄₈″ × 2⁷⁄₈″ square in half once diagonally to make 2 half-square triangles (8 total) (A). (You will need 7 for each block—84 total for the quilt.)

From *each* assorted medium or dark print #2 fabric:

Cut each 2⁷⁄₈″ × 2⁷⁄₈″ square in half once diagonally to make 2 half-square triangles (4 total) (A). (You will need 3 for each block—36 total for the quilt.)

From *each* assorted medium or dark print #3 fabric:

Cut each 2⁷⁄₈″ × 2⁷⁄₈″ square in half once diagonally to make 2 half-square triangles (2 total) (A). (You will need 2 for each block—24 total for the quilt.)

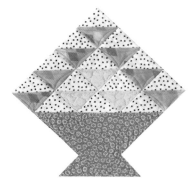

Cut the 6⅞" × 6⅞" square in half once diagonally to make 2 half-square triangles (2 total) (B). (You will need 1 for each block—12 total for the quilt.)

From the assorted setting-square and setting-triangle fabrics:

Cut 6 squares, 10½" × 10½".

Cut 3 squares, 17" × 17". Cut in half twice diagonally to make 4 quarter-square triangles (12 total). You will have 2 triangles left over.

Cut 2 squares, 11" × 11". Cut each square in half once diagonally to make 2 half-square triangles (4 total).

From the inner-border fabric:

Cut 2 strips, 1¼" × 40". Crosscut into

1 strip, 1¼" × 24",

4 strips, 1¼" × 5½", and

4 strips, 1¼" × 6¼".

Cut 7 strips, 1¼" × 40".

From the second- and outer-border fabric:

Cut 2 strips, 1¼" × 40". Crosscut into

1 strip, 1¼" × 24", and

4 strips, 1¼" × 5½".

Cut 7 strips, 1¼" × 40".

Cut 7 strips, 4" × 40".

From the third-border fabric:

Cut 1 strip, 1¼" × 24".

Cut 7 strips, 1¼" × 40".

From the binding fabric:

Cut 7 strips, 3" × 40".

From the hanging-sleeve fabric:

Cut 2 strips, 8½" × 40".

making the lap/large wall quilt

1. Follow the instructions for Making the Blocks (page 74). Make 12 blocks.

2. Arrange the blocks, the 10½" setting squares, the quarter-square side-setting triangles, and the half-square corner-setting triangles in diagonal rows, as shown in the assembly diagram. Assemble and trim the quilt top as described in Assembling the Quilt, Steps 2–4 (page 75).

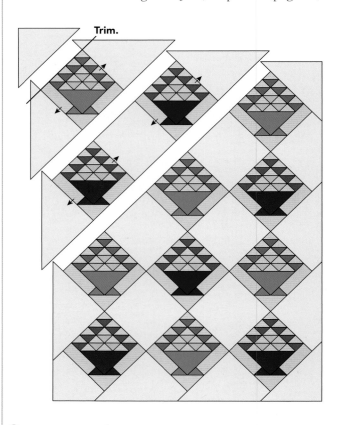

3. Arrange the 1¼" × 24" second-border strip, the 1¼" × 24" third-border strip, and the 4" × 24" outer-border strip, as shown. Sew the strips together to make a 5½" × 24" strip set; press. Cut the strip set into four 4"-wide segments and four 1¼"-wide segments.

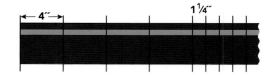

Cut 4 segments 4" wide and 4 segments 1¼" wide.

4. Arrange a 4″-wide segment from Step 3, a $1\frac{1}{4}″ \times 5\frac{1}{2}″$ third-border strip, a $1\frac{1}{4}″$-wide segment from Step 3, and a $1\frac{1}{4}″ \times 5\frac{1}{2}″$ inner-border strip, as shown. Sew the segments and strips together. Press. Sew a $1\frac{1}{4}″ \times 6\frac{1}{4}″$ inner-border strip to the side of the unit, as shown. Press. Make 4.

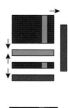

Make 4.

5. Cut one $1\frac{1}{4}″$ x 40″ inner-border strip in half to make 2 strips $1\frac{1}{4}″$ x 20″. Sew each half strip to an inner-border $1\frac{1}{4}″$ x 40″ strip end to end to make 2 strips $1\frac{1}{4}″$ x 60″. Press. Sew together the remaining $1\frac{1}{4}″$ x 40″ inner-border strips end to end in pairs to make 2 strips $1\frac{1}{4}″$ x 80″.

6. Repeat Step 5 for the $1\frac{1}{4}″$ x 40″ second-border strips, the 4″ x 40″ outer-border strips, and the $1\frac{1}{4}″$ x 40″ third-border strips.

7. Arrange and sew together the long strips from Steps 5 and 6 to make 2 strip sets $6\frac{1}{4}″ \times 60″$ and 2 strip sets $6\frac{1}{4}″ \times 80″$.

8. Refer to Borders with Cornerstones (page 15) and to the assembly diagram. Measure and trim border units for the sides, top, and bottom of the quilt. Sew the side border units to the sides of the quilt. Press the seams toward the border units. Sew units from Step 4 to opposite ends of the top and bottom border units and sew them to the top and bottom of the quilt. Press.

9. Finish the quilt as described in Preparing Your Quilt for Quilting, Quilting Your Quilt, and Finishing Your Quilt (pages 16–21).

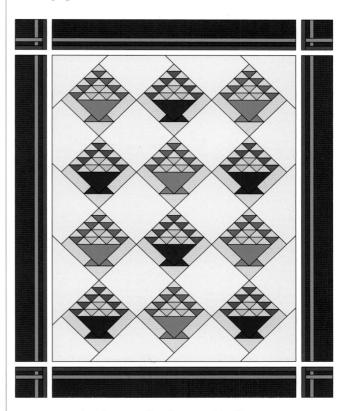

Lap/large wall quilt assembly diagram

CREATIVE OPTIONS

Wow! My creative group of quilters outdid themselves with clever options for this quilt. For instance, Carla Zimmermann introduced a sawtooth border—a choice much in keeping with the traditional dark background and overall palette of her quilt *Amish Baskets* (page 82).

Annette Barca decided to forgo the on-point setting and instead arranged six Gathering Moments blocks in a straight set with lattice strips and cornerstones. See her quilt *Amelia Goes Trick or Treating* on page 82. Amelia is M'Liss's dachshund.

You may also notice that Annette omitted the inner set of small triangles in each Gathering Moments block. John James did the same, taking advantage of the resulting large space to feature a collection of fruit and vegetable novelty prints that fill his *Bountiful Baskets* (page 81) to the brim.

Susie Kincy loves embellishment, and her nine-block version of the Gathering Moments on point quilt is a visual, textural delight. She also omitted the small inner triangles and instead filled her Gathering Moments baskets with lace (machine-embroidered and real), ribbons, vintage buttons, and other delicate details. For a final decorative touch, she inserted prairie points—not on the very edge of the quilt, but between the inner and outer borders.

Detail of novelty fabric in *Bountiful Baskets*

Detail of embellished Gathering Moments block in *Grandmother's Button Basket*

Detail of Susie's prairie-point inserts

BOUNTIFUL BASKETS,
55½″ × 70″.

*Pieced by John James, machine
quilted by Barbara Dau, 2007.*

GRANDMOTHER'S BUTTON BASKETS,
58″ × 58″.

*Pieced, embroidered, and embellished
by Susie Kincy, machine quilted by
Barbara Dau, 2007.*

AMELIA GOES TRICK OR TREATING,
37″ × 49″.

Pieced by Annette Barca, machine quilted by Barbara Dau, 2007.

AMISH BASKETS,
58″ × 72″.

Pieced by Carla Zimmermann, machine quilted by Kim McKinnon, 2007.

Union Square

MIRACLES HAPPEN, designed and made by M'Liss Rae Hawley, machine quilted by Barbara Dau, 2007.

Finished quilt: 100½″ × 107½″

Finished block: 12″ × 12″

The small pieces in this star-based block lend themselves beautifully to scraps, and the block looks good in either a straight or on-point setting. Therefore, I couldn't resist giving you two versions of this pattern. As you can see, I placed the blocks in *Miracles Happen* on point, alternating them with pink setting squares cut from four different pink prints. The setting triangles are red, again cut from four different prints, and the quilt is finished with a series of four borders, making it large enough for a queen- or king-sized bed. You'll find the smaller, straight-set version on page 90.

If you look closely at *Miracles Happen,* you'll discover that I used "orphans" from my embroidery basket for the center square in some blocks. Yes, these are embroidery scraps! These are thread-color stitch outs, design checks, and other test pieces, duplicates, and embroideries that did not make it into other projects. I had to carefully recut the squares on the bias to accommodate the on-point setting. The challenge was centering the design, but I think the results were worth it.

materials

Yardage is based on 40″-wide fabric.

- ¼ yard *each* of 20 assorted fabrics for block background (A, B, C)

- 1 square 4½″ × 4½″ *each* of 20 assorted fabrics for star centers (D)

- 2 squares 5¼″ × 5¼″ *each* of 20 assorted print #1 for large star points (A)

- 1 square 5¼″ × 5¼″ *each* of 20 assorted print #2 for center triangles (A)

- 4 squares 2⅞″ × 2⅞″ *each* of 20 assorted print #3 for small star points (B)

- ½ yard *each* of 4 assorted fabrics for setting squares

- ¾ yard *each* of 4 assorted fabrics for setting triangles

- ¾ yard of fabric for inner border

- 1⅝ yards of fabric for second border

- 1⅝ yards of fabric for third border (If using a directional print [refer to page 85], you will need 3½ yards.)

- 1 yard of fabric for outer border

- 1⅛ yards of fabric for binding

- 9¾ yards of fabric for backing

- ¾ yard of fabric for hanging sleeve

- 109″ × 116″ piece of batting

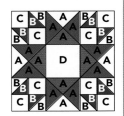

Block diagram

cutting

Cut strips on the crosswise grain (from selvage to selvage).

From each assorted background fabric:

Cut 1 square, 5¼″ × 5¼″. Cut the square twice diagonally to make 4 quarter-square triangles (A). (You will need 4 for each block—80 total for the quilt.)

Cut 4 squares, 2⅞″ × 2⅞″. Cut each square once diagonally to make 2 half-square triangles (B). (You will need 8 for each block—160 total for the quilt.)

Cut 4 squares, 2½″ × 2½″ (C). (You will need 4 for each block—80 total for the quilt.)

From each assorted print #1 fabric:

Cut each 5¼″ × 5¼″ square in half twice diagonally to make 4 quarter-square triangles (A). (You will need 8 for each block—160 total for the quilt.)

From each assorted print #2 fabric:

Cut the 5¼″ × 5¼″ square in half twice diagonally to make 4 half-square triangles (A). (You will need 4 for each block—80 total for the quilt.)

From each assorted print #3 fabric:

Cut each 2⅞″ × 2⅞″ square in half once diagonally to make 2 half-square triangles (B). (You will need 8 for each block—160 total for the quilt.)

From each assorted setting-square fabric:

Cut 3 squares, 12½″ × 12½″ (12 total).

From each assorted setting-triangle fabric:

Cut 1 square, 20½″ × 20½″. Cut in half twice diagonally to make 4 quarter-square triangles (16 total). (You will need 13 triangles.)

From each of 2 assorted setting-triangle fabrics:

Cut 1 square, 12½″ × 12½″. Cut in half once diagonally to make 2 half-square triangles (4 total).

From the inner-border fabric:

Cut 4 strips, 2″ × 40″.

Cut 5 strips, 2½″ × 40″.

From the second-border fabric:

Cut 4 strips, 4¼″ × 40″.

Cut 5 strips, 6½″ × 40″.

From the third-border fabric:

Cut 5 strips, 3¼″ × 40″.

Cut 6 strips, 5½″ × 40″.

From the outer-border fabric:

Cut 11 strips, 2½″ × 40″.

From the binding fabric:

Cut 11 strips, 3″ × 40″.

From the hanging-sleeve fabric:

Cut 3 strips, 8½″ × 40″.

FOLLOWING "DIRECTIONS"!

If you use an obviously directional fabric as a border, such as my Kimono Art II crane fabric I used for the second border of my quilt, you'll need to purchase additional fabric to allow for cutting lengthwise strips.

I cut some strips crosswise and some strips lengthwise to keep the cranes right side up in this directional border fabric.

making the blocks

1. With right sides together, sew a print #1 quarter-square triangle A to a background quarter-square triangle A along one short edge, as shown. Press. Make 4 matching units.

Make 4.

2. Repeat Step 1 using a matching print #1 quarter-square triangle A and a print #2 quarter-square triangle A. Press. Make 4 matching units.

Make 4.

3. Sew the units from Step 1 and Step 2 together. Press. Make 4.

Make 4.

4. Sew a print #3 half-square triangle B to a background half-square triangle B along the long edges. Press. Make 8 matching units.

Make 8.

5. Arrange and sew 2 units from Step 4 and 2 matching 2½″ background squares (C) together, as shown. Press. Make 4.

Make 4.

6. Arrange and sew together the 4 units from Step 3, the 4 units from Step 5, and one 4½″ center square (D). Press.

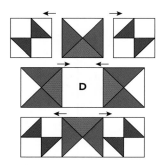

7. Repeat Steps 1–6 to make a total of 20 blocks.

assembling the quilt

The side and corner triangles are cut oversized so that the blocks appear to float. You will square up the quilt top after it is assembled.

1. Arrange the blocks, the 12½″ setting squares, the quarter-square side-setting triangles, and the half-square corner-setting triangles in diagonal rows, as shown in the assembly diagram.

2. Sew the blocks, setting squares, and side-setting triangles together into diagonal rows. Press the seams in alternating directions from row to row.

3. Sew the rows together. Press. Trim the dog ears at each corner. Press the seams toward the triangles.

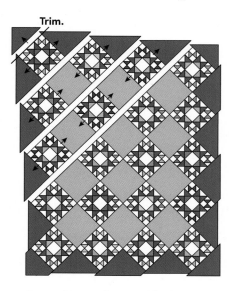

Queen/king quilt assembly diagram

4. Square up the quilt top, measuring 1⅜″ from the corners of the blocks to trim the side and corner triangles.

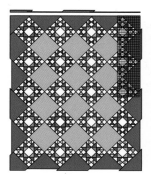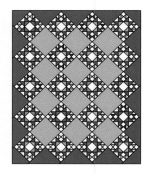

5. Refer to Squared Borders (page 14). Measure, trim, and sew 2″-wide inner-border strips to the top and bottom of the quilt, piecing the strips as necessary. Press the seams toward the border. Repeat to sew 2½″-wide inner-border strips to the sides, piecing the strips as necessary. Press.

6. Repeat Step 5 to measure, trim, and sew the 4¼″-wide second-border strips to the top and bottom of the quilt and the 6½″-wide second-border strips to the sides, piecing the strips as necessary. Press the seams toward the second border.

7. Repeat Step 5 to measure, trim, and sew the 3¼″-wide third-border strips to the top and bottom of the quilt and the 5½″-wide third-border strips to the sides, piecing the strips as necessary. Press the seams toward the third border.

8. Repeat Step 5 to measure, trim, and sew the 2½″-wide outer-border strips to the top, bottom, and sides of the quilt, piecing the strips as necessary. Press the seams toward the outer border.

finishing the quilt

Refer to Preparing Your Quilt for Quilting, Quilting Your Quilt, and Finishing Your Quilt (pages 16–21).

1. Piece the backing as described on page 17.

2. Layer the quilt top, batting, and backing; baste.

3. Hand or machine quilt as desired.

4. Use the 3″-wide strips to bind the edges of the quilt.

5. Add a hanging sleeve and label if desired.

Union Square: Pillows and Pillowcases

MIRACLES HAPPEN PILLOW
AND PILLOWCASES,
made by M'Liss Rae Hawley, 2007.

Here are some decorative accents
to complete your Union Square
bedding ensemble.

Finished pillow size: 16″ × 16″

Finished pillowcase size:
32½″ × 20″

materials

Yardage is based on fabric that is 40½″ wide.

PILLOW

Amounts shown are for one pillow.

- ¼ yard for block background (A, B, C)

- 1 square 4½″ × 4½″ for star center (D)

- 2 squares 5¼″ × 5¼″ print #1 for large star points (A)

- 1 square 5¼″ × 5¼″ print #2 for center triangles (A)

- 4 squares 2⅞″ × 2⅞″ print #3 for small star points (B)

- ¼ yard of fabric for the border

- ½ yard of fabric for the backing

- 16″ × 16″ pillow form

- ⅝ yard of lining fabric (optional)

- 20″ × 20″ piece of batting (optional)

PILLOWCASES

Amounts shown are for two pillowcases.

- 1¾ yards of pillowcase fabric

- ¾ yard of cuff fabric

cutting

Cut strips on the crosswise grain (from selvage to selvage).

PILLOW

From the border fabric:

Cut 2 strips, 2½″ × 12½″.

Cut 2 strips, 2½″ × 16½″.

From the backing fabric:

Cut 2 pieces, 16½″ × 10½″.

PILLOWCASES

From the pillowcase fabric:

Cut 2 pieces, 28″ × 40½″.

From the cuff fabric:

Cut 2 strips, 11″ × 40½″.

assembling the pillow

1. Use the instructions for Cutting prints #1, #2, and #3 (page 84) and for Making the Blocks, Steps 1–6 (pages 85–86) to make a Union Square block.

2. Sew a 2½″-wide border strip to the top and bottom of the block. Press. Repeat to sew 2½″-wide borders to the sides. Press.

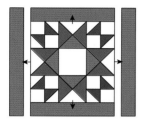

Assembly diagram

Note: If you wish, you can layer and quilt the pillow top before assembling it into a pillow. You'll need a 20″ × 20″ square each of batting or diaper flannel and lining fabric. Refer to Preparing Your Quilt for Quilting (page 16) and Quilting Your Quilt (page 17) for guidance as needed. Trim the batting and lining even with the pillow top after quilting.

3. Fold under a ¼″ hem along one long edge of each 16½″ × 10½″ backing piece. Press. Fold under another ¼″. Press and stitch along the folded edge.

4. With right sides up, place one backing piece over the other so the hemmed edges overlap, making the backing piece the same size as the pillow top. Baste the backing pieces together at the top and bottom where they overlap.

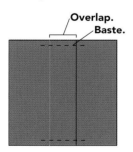

Overlap.
Baste.

5. With right sides together, align and pin the pillow top to the backing. Sew around the outside edges with a ¼″-wide seam. Remove the basting, trim the corners, and turn the pillow cover right side out. Press before inserting the pillow form.

assembling the pillowcase

1. With right sides together, fold an 11″ × 40½″ strip of cuff fabric in half lengthwise. Press. Make 2.

2. Align the long raw edges of a folded cuff with the long raw edges on the right side of a 28″ × 40½″ piece of case fabric; pin. Sew the cuff to the case with a ¼″ seam. Zigzag or serge the raw edges to keep them from fraying. Press the seams away from the cuff. Topstitch ⅛″ from the seam joining the cuff to the case on the case fabric to finish. Make 2.

3. With right sides together, fold each unit from Step 2 in half, as shown. Sew along the long raw edges and the raw, uncuffed edges with a ¼″ seam. Zigzag or serge the raw edges to keep them from fraying. Make 2.

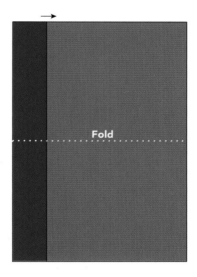

Fold

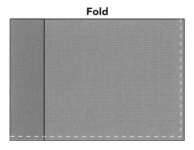

Fold

Make 2.

4. Turn each pillowcase right side out. To finish, topstitch on the case fabric ⅛″ from the seam, joining the cuff to the case.

Union Square: Version II

ELEGANCE IN UNION SQUARE, pieced by Vicki DeGraaf, machine quilted by Barbara Dau, 2007.

Finished quilt: 56½″ × 70″

Finished block: 12″ × 12″

materials

Yardage is based on 40″-wide fabric.

◆ ¼ yard *each* of 12 assorted fabrics for block background (A, B, C)

◆ 1 square 4½″ × 4½″ *each* of 12 assorted fabrics for star centers (D)

◆ 2 squares 5¼″ × 5¼″ *each* of 12 assorted print #1 for large star points (A)

◆ 1 square 5¼″ × 5¼″ *each* of 12 assorted print #2 for center triangles (A)

◆ 4 squares 2⅞″ × 2⅞″ *each* of 12 assorted print #3 for small star points (B)

◆ ¾ yard of fabric for lattice strips

◆ ¼ yard of fabric for cornerstones

◆ 1½ yards of fabric for outer border

◆ ¾ yard of fabric for binding

◆ 4½ yards of fabric for backing

◆ ⅝ yard of fabric for hanging sleeve

◆ 65″ × 78″ piece of batting

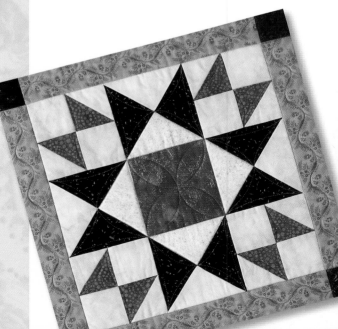

traight-set blocks, separated by lattice and framed by a single wide border, result in a lap quilt that can double as a twin-bed coverlet. Vicki DeGraaf used a wide range of beautiful gold, brown, and black fabrics, many covered with metallic thread.

cutting

Cut strips on the crosswise grain (from selvage to selvage).

From *each* assorted background fabric:

Cut 1 square, 5¼" × 5¼". Cut the square twice diagonally to make 4 quarter-square triangles (A). (You will need 4 for each block—48 total for the quilt.)

Cut 4 squares, 2⅞" × 2⅞". Cut each square once diagonally to make 2 half-square triangles (B). (You will need 8 for each block—96 total for the quilt.)

Cut 4 squares, 2½" × 2½" (C). (You will need 4 for each block—48 total for the quilt.)

From the lattice fabric:

Cut 11 strips, 2" × 40". Crosscut into 31 strips, 2" × 12½".

From the cornerstone fabric:

Cut 1 strip, 2" × 40". Crosscut into 20 squares, 2" × 2".

From the outer-border fabric:

Cut 6 strips, 7½" × 40".

From the binding fabric:

Cut 7 strips, 3" × 40".

From the hanging-sleeve fabric:

Cut 2 strips, 8½" × 40".

making the lap quilt

1. Follow the instructions for Cutting prints #1, #2, and #3 (page 84) and Making the Blocks, Steps 1–6 (pages 85–86). Make 12 blocks.

2. Arrange 3 blocks and 4 lattice strips 2" × 12½", alternating them as shown in the assembly diagram. Sew the blocks and strips together. Press the seams toward the lattice strips. Make 4.

3. Arrange and sew 3 lattice strips 2" × 12½" and 4 cornerstones 2" × 2", alternating them as shown in the assembly diagram. Sew the strips and cornerstones together. Press the seams toward the lattice strips. Make 5.

4. Arrange the rows from Steps 2 and 3, alternating them as shown in the assembly diagram. Sew the rows together. Press the seams toward the lattice/cornerstone rows.

5. Refer to Squared Borders (page 14). Measure, trim, and sew 7½"-wide outer-border strips to the top and bottom of the quilt, piecing the strips as necessary. Press the seams toward the border. Repeat to sew 7½"-wide outer-border strips to the sides, piecing the strips as necessary. Press.

6. Finish the quilt as described in Preparing Your Quilt for Quilting, Quilting Your Quilt, and Finishing Your Quilt (pages 16–21).

Lap quilt assembly diagram

STARS WATCH OVER CIVIL WAR BATTLEFIELD,
56″ × 70″.

*Pieced by Carla Zimmermann, machine quilted
by Arlene Anderson, 2007.*

LOOK AT ALL THOSE BLUES,
50″ × 50″.

*Pieced by Annette Barca, machine quilted
by Barbara Dau, 2007.*

ROSES IN UNION SQUARE,
60˝ × 73˝.

*Pieced by John and Louise James,
machine quilted by Barbara Dau, 2007.*

PERFECT POINTS,
50½˝ × 62½˝.

*Pieced and machine quilted by
Barbara Dau, 2007.*

Resources

sources and information for products referenced

For a list of other fine books from C&T Publishing, ask for a free catalog:

C&T Publishing, Inc.
P.O. Box 1456
Lafayette, CA 94549
(800) 284-1114
Email: ctinfo@ctpub.com
Website: www.ctpub.com

C&T Publishing's professional photography services are now available to the public. Visit us at www.ctmediaservices.com.

For fat quarters and other quilting supplies:

Cotton Patch
1025 Brown Ave.
Lafayette, CA 94549
(800) 835-4418 or
(925) 283-7883
Email: CottonPa@aol.com
Website: www.quiltusa.com

Island Fabrics Etc.
www.islandfabrics.com

Note: Fabrics used in the quilts shown may not be currently available, as fabric manufacturers keep most fabrics in print for only a short time.

For information about thread:
Robison-Anton Textile Company
www.robison-anton.com

For information about thread and stabilizer:
Sulky of America
www.sulky.com

To locate your nearest Husqvarna Viking dealer:
Husqvarna Viking
www.husqvarnaviking.com

For more on the color wheel and how it works, refer to:
Get Creative with M'Liss Rae Hawley, C&T Publishing, 2005, page 10.

embroidery collections

These and other embroidery collections are available at your participating local Husqvarna Viking and Pfaff sewing machine dealers.

Scrappy Quilts

Kimono Art, by M'Liss Rae Hawley, Disk Part #756 259800, *inspira* collection, multiformat CD-ROM

Kimono Art II, by M'Liss Rae Hawley, Disk Part #620 037296, *inspira* collection, multiformat CD-ROM

My Favorite Quilt Designs, by M'Liss Rae Hawley, Disk Part #756 253300, *inspira* collection, multiformat CD-ROM

Spring View, by M'Liss Rae Hawley, Disk Part #756 255100, *inspira* collection, multiformat CD-ROM

Textures & Techniques with M'Liss, by M'Liss Rae Hawley, Husqvarna Viking Embroidery 181

Quilting with M'Liss, by M'Liss Rae Hawley, Husqvarna Viking Embroidery 175

Ethno 308

American, Disk Part #556 255900

Paper Lanterns, Disk Part #756 104500

Teapots, EZ Sew Designs, Disk Part #756 101600

Celebrate! by Marna, Disk Part #756 255700

French Café, by Agneta Mars, #412 8063-01

Petite Paisley, by Margit Grimm, #412 8079-01

Playing Around, *inspira*, #6200324-96

About the Author

M'Liss Rae Hawley is an accomplished quilting teacher, lecturer, embroidery and textile designer, and best-selling author. She conducts workshops and seminars throughout the world. As the author of 10 books, including *Phenomenal Fat Quarter Quilts* (2004), *Get Creative! with M'Liss Rae Hawley* (2005), *M'Liss Rae Hawley's Round Robin Renaissance* (2006), *M'Liss Rae Hawley's Mariner's Medallion Quilts* (2006), *M'Liss Rae Hawley's Fat Quarter Quilts* (2007), *Make Your First Quilt with M'Liss Rae Hawley* (2007), and the originator of numerous innovative designs, M'Liss is constantly seeking new boundaries to challenge her students while imparting her enthusiasm and love for the art of quilting.

Although she is in production for her new PBS television series, *M'Liss's Quilting World*, M'Liss continues to create fabric exclusively for Jo-Ann Fabrics (with coordinating embroidery collections), write books, and create patterns for many magazines. M'Liss is the quilting spokesperson for Husqvarna Viking and Robison-Anton Textile Company. She likes to break quilting down to the basics to show students that quilting can be easy and fun at any level of skill.

M'Liss and her husband, Michael, live on Whidbey Island, Washington, in a filbert orchard. Michael is also a best-selling author and the recently retired sheriff of Island County. Their son, Alexander, is a sergeant in the U.S. Marine Corps, currently serving overseas, and their daughter, Adrienne, a recent graduate of Seattle University, is a volunteer firefighter and is serving in AmeriCorps. Michael and M'Liss share their home with seven dachshunds and four cats.

M'LISS'S QUILT GROUP—
Back row (from left): Carla Zimmermann, Anastasia Riordan, Leslie Rommann, John James, Barbara Dau, Annette Barca.
Front row (from left): Lucia Pan, Vicki DeGraaf, M'Liss Rae Hawley, Susie Kincy, Peggy Johnson.
Not pictured: Louise James and Marie Miller.

Other Titles by M'Liss

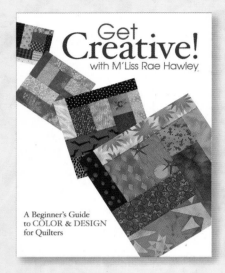

Get Creative!
with M'Liss Rae Hawley

A Beginner's Guide to COLOR & DESIGN for Quilters

M'Liss Rae Hawley
Phenomenal fat quarter quilts

new Projects with Tips to Inspire & Enhance Your Quiltmaking

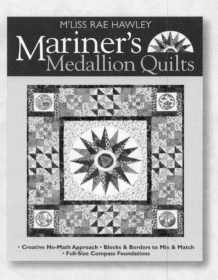

M'LISS RAE HAWLEY
Mariner's Medallion Quilts

• Creative No-Math Approach • Blocks & Borders to Mix & Match
• Full-Size Compass Foundations

M'Liss Rae Hawley's
Round·Robin Renaissance

5 Fresh Approaches for Creative Expression
30 Traditional Quilt Blocks • Fun, Foolproof Process

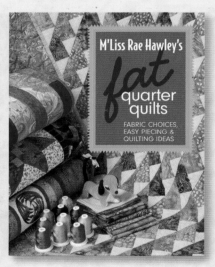

M'Liss Rae Hawley's
fat quarter quilts

FABRIC CHOICES, EASY PIECING & QUILTING IDEAS

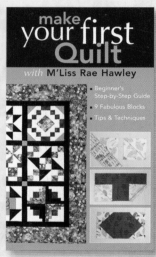

make your first Quilt
with M'Liss Rae Hawley

• Beginner's Step-by-Step Guide
• 9 Fabulous Blocks
• Tips & Techniques

M'Liss's Quilting World
Bring Color and Creativity into Your Life